In memory of Denise Adele Jefferson, 1944–2010

And for Nancy Gist and Christine Carter Lynch

Negroland

Also by Margo Jefferson

On Michael Jackson

Negroland

A Memoir

Margo Jefferson

GRANTA

Granta Publications, 12 Addison Avenue, London W11 4QR

First published in Great Britain by Granta Books in 2016

First published in the United States by in 2015 by Pantheon Books, a division of Penguin Random House LLC, New York.

A CIP catalogue record for this book is available from the British Library.

3 5 7 9 10 8 6 4 2

ISBN 978 1 78378 302 1 (trade paperback)

ISBN 978 1 78378 303 8 (ebook)

Book design by M. Kristen-Bearse

Offset by M Rules

Printed and bound by CPI Group (UK) Ltd, Croydon, CR0 4YY

www.grantabooks.com

Negroland

I was taught to avoid showing off.

I was taught to distinguish myself through presentation, not declaration, to excel through deeds and manners, not showing off.

But isn't all memoir a form of showing off?

In my Negroland childhood, this was a perilous business.

Negroland is my name for a small region of Negro America where residents were sheltered by a certain amount of privilege and plenty. Children in Negroland were warned that few Negroes enjoyed privilege or plenty and that most whites would be glad to see them returned to indigence, deference, and subservience. Children there were taught that most other Negroes ought to be emulating us when too many of them (out of envy or ignorance) went on behaving in ways that encouraged racial prejudice.

Too many Negroes, it was said, showed off the wrong things: their loud voices, their brash and garish ways; their gift for popular music and dance, for sports rather than the humanities and sciences. Most white people were on the lookout, we were told, for what they called these basic racial traits. But most white people were also on the lookout for a too-bold display by us of *their* kind of accomplishments, *their* privilege and plenty, what they considered *their* racial traits. You were never to act undignified in their presence, but neither were you to act flamboyant.

Showing off was permitted, even encouraged, only if the result reflected well on your family, their friends, and your collective ancestors.

So here I am, age four, at a children's club talent show, in the wings of an auditorium with other excited Jack and Jillers. While we are being gently and firmly shushed, I break away and stride onto the stage. My five-year-old friend is performing her recitation. I step in front of her, turn around, and tell the adult seated at the piano, "Keep playing that music." He obeys; I turn back to the audience and do my notion of a dance for a few minutes. I hear the adults exclaim and laugh appreciatively. I've charmed them because I have a reputation for being bright and spirited; even my friend's mother is indulgent. I don't recall my friend's reaction—why should I? I was out to obliterate her.

I could take adult indulgence too far when my need to shine blurred my sense of the occasion. At a dinner party not long after, where the adults were more interested in each other than in children, I waited for a break in their talk, then announced, "Sometimes I forget to wipe myself."

The laughter came, but only after a short silence, and I saw the guests looking at each other before they looked at me. I realized I was being more tolerated than appreciated, and it came to me that repeating such a statement—showing off in public what's done in private—would always bring reproof.

So I grew. And as I grew I learned that in the world beyond family and family friends, your mistakes—bad manners, poor taste, an excess of high spirits—could put you, your parents, and your people at risk.

All of you could be designated, at a stroke and for life, vulgar, coarse, and inferior.

Clever of me to become a critic. We critics scrutinize and show off to a higher end. For a greater good. Our manners, our tastes, our declarations are welcomed.

Superior for life. Except when we're not. Except when we're dismissed or denounced as envious and petty; as derivatives and dependents by nature. Second class for life.

That's the generic version of a story. Here's the specific version: the midwestern, midcentury story of a little girl, one of two born to an attractive couple pleased with their lives and achievements, wanting the best for their children and wanting their children to be among the best.

To be successful, professionally and personally.

And to be happy.

Children always find ways to subvert while they're busy complying. This child's method of subversion? She would achieve success, but she would treat it like a concession she'd been forced to make. For unto whomsoever much is given, of her shall be much required. She came to feel that too much had been required of her. She would have her revenge. She would insist on an inner life regulated by despair.

The story she constructs is this: There was a girl, once upon a time and in your time. She embraced her life up to a point, then rejected it, and from that rejection have come all her difficulties. She comes to feel that her life has gone wrong. Some of this is the usual thwarted ambition—she's good, quite good, at her profession. She should have been outstanding. She is, by some measures, but she's not phenomenal. She knows she's privileged to be a writer. She should love what she does. But she doesn't. Much of the time she convinces herself that she hates writing and therefore feels hate toward it. About love and sex she should have been adventurous, not wary. How does someone like this, so often ashamed of what she is, always ashamed of what she lacks, write about herself?

I'm going to change my tone now. I think it's too easy to recount unhappy memories when you write about yourself. You bask in your own innocence. You revere your grief. You arrange your angers at their most becoming angles.

I don't want this kind of indulgence to dominate my memories.

And (I was taught) you don't tell your secrets to strangers— certainly not secrets that expose error, weakness, failure.

Nothing is just personal. And all readers are strangers. Right now I'm overwhelmed by trying to calculate, imagine, what these readers might expect of me; reject, demand, deny; how this one will insist, as that one resists . . .

So let me turn back, subdue my individual self, and enter history.

I'm a chronicler of Negroland, a participant-observer, an elegist, dissenter and admirer; sometime expatriate, ongoing interlocutor.

I call it Negroland because I still find "Negro" a word of wonders, glorious and terrible. A word for runaway slave posters and civil rights proclamations; for social constructs and street corner flaunts. A tonal-language word whose meaning shifts as setting and context shift, as history twists, lurches, advances, and stagnates. As capital letters appear to enhance its dignity; as other nomenclatures arise to challenge its primacy.

I call it Negroland because "Negro" dominated our history for so long; because I lived with its meanings and intimations for so long; because they were essential to my first discoveries of what race meant, or, as we now say, how race was constructed.

For nearly two hundred years we in Negroland have called ourselves all manner of things. Like

the colored aristocracy
the colored elite
the colored 400
the 400
the blue vein society
the big families, the old families, the old settlers, the
    pioneers

Negro society, black society
the Negro, the black, the African-American upper class or
    elite.

I was born in 1947, and my generation, like its predecessors,
was taught that since our achievements received little notice or
credit from white America, we were not to discuss our faults,
lapses, or uncertainties in public. (Even now I shy away from the
word "failings.") Even the least of them would be turned against
the race. Most white people made no room for the doctrine of
"human, all too human": our imperfections were sub- or provisionally human.

For my generation the motto was still: Achievement. Invul-
nerability. Comportment.

Part of me dreads revealing anything in these pages except
our drive to excellence. But I dread the constricted expression
that comes from that. And we're prone to being touchy. Self-
righteously smug and snobbish. So let me begin in a quiet, clinical way.

I was born into the Chicago branch of Negroland. My father
was a doctor, a pediatrician, and for some years head of pediatrics at Provident, the nation's oldest black hospital. My mother
was a social worker who left her job when she married, and
throughout my childhood she was a full-time wife, mother, and
socialite. But where did they come from to get there? And which
clubs and organizations did they join to seal their membership
in this world?

A brief vita of the author.

Margo Jefferson:
Ancestors: (In chronological order): slaves and slaveholders
    in Virginia, Kentucky, and Mississippi; farmers, musi-

cians, butlers, construction crew supervisors, teachers, beauticians and maids, seamstresses and dressmakers, engineers, policewomen, real estate businesswomen, lawyers, judges, doctors and social workers

Father's fraternity: Kappa Alpha Psi

Mother's (and sister's) sorority: Delta Sigma Theta

Parents' national clubs: the Boulé (father); the Northeasterners (mother)

Sister's and my national clubs: Jack and Jill; the Co-Ettes

Local clubs, schools, and camps will be named as we go along. Skin color and hair will be described, evaluated too, along with other racialized physical traits. Questions inevitably will arise. Among them: How does one—how do you, how do I—parse class, race, family, and temperament? How many kinds of deprivation are there? What is the compass of privilege? What has made and maimed me?

Here are some of this group's founding categories, the oppositions and distinctions they came to live by.

Northerner / Southerner
house slave / field hand
free black / slave black
free black / free mulatto
skilled worker / unskilled worker (free or slave)
owns property / owns none
reads and writes fluently / reads a little but does not write /
    reads and writes a little / neither reads nor writes
descends from African and Indian royalty / descends from
    African obscurities / descends from upper-class whites /

descends from lower-class whites / descends from no
whites at all

White Americans have always known how to develop aris-
tocracies from local resources, however scant. British grocers
arrive on the *Mayflower* and become founding fathers. German
laborers emigrate to Chicago and become slaughterhouse kings.
Women of equally modest origins marry these men or their
rivals or their betters and become social arbiters.

We did the same. "Colored society" was originally a mé-
lange of

men and women who were given favorable treatment,
    money, property, and even freedom by well-born Cauca-
    sian owners, employers, and parents;
men and women who bought their freedom with hard cash
    and hard labor;
men, women, and children bought and freed by slavery-
    hating whites or Negro friends and relatives;
men and women descended from free Negroes, hence born
    free.

They learned their letters and their manners; they learned
skilled trades (barber, caterer, baker, jeweler, machinist, tailor,
dressmaker); they were the best-trained servants in the better white homes and hotels; they bought real estate; published
newspapers; established schools and churches; formed clubs
and mutual aid societies; took care to marry among themselves.
Some arrived from Haiti alongside whites fleeing Toussaint
L'Ouverture's black revolution: their ranks included free mulattoes and slaves who, after some pretense of loyalty, found it easy
to desert their former masters and go into the business of upward

mobility. From New Orleans to New York, men and women of mixed blood insistently established their primacy.

I've fallen into a mocking tone that feels prematurely disloyal. There were antebellum founders of Negroland who triumphed through resolve and principled intelligence.

A few examples:

James Forten of Philadelphia, abolitionist and entrepreneur. Born to free Negro parents, he started work in a sail-making firm at age eight, became the foreman at twenty and the owner at twenty-three, running the firm so well that it made him one of the richest men, *black or white,* in the city. He invented a sail-handling device, refused to sell rigging to slave-trading ships, organized against slavery and colonization, fought attempts to curtail the rights of free blacks, and supplied much-needed funds to help William Lloyd Garrison start *The Liberator.*

Frances Jackson Coppin, educator. Born in Washington, D.C., she remained a slave until age twelve. Her Negro grandfather bought the freedom of all his children except her mother, who was left enslaved because she'd had Frances by a white man. When an aunt bought her freedom, she worked as a servant in Massachusetts, then Rhode Island; using her salary to employ a tutor, she made her way through high school and then Oberlin College. There she started a school for escaped slaves while successfully completing the men's course of study in Latin, Greek, and higher mathematics. She became an educator— the first Negro woman to head a high school with a classical curriculum—who burned, as she told Frederick Douglass, "to see my race lifted out of the mire of ignorance, weakness and degradation; no longer to sit in obscure corners and devour the scraps of knowledge which his superiors flung at him."[*]

* What had once been the Douglass High School in Baltimore, Maryland, became Coppin State University in 1926.

———

Negro exceptionalism had its ugly side: pioneers who advanced through resolve, intelligence, and exploiting their own.

Anthony Johnson was born in Angola and brought to Virginia in 1621; he began plantation life as an indentured servant before slavery was firmly established. Mary, another Negro servant, became his wife. They produced four children and completed their term of service; Johnson bought 250 acres of land in 1640. (The same year, a black indentured servant who'd fled was caught and sentenced to "serve his said master . . . for the time of his natural life.") Anthony and Mary increased their 250 acres to 550, and acquired cattle and indentured servants. In 1654, one of those servants, the Negro John Casor, accused Johnson of wanting to enslave him and left, going to work for a white landowner willing to treat him as an indentured servant. Johnson took the white landowner to court, won his case on appeal, and took Casor back into servitude for life, thus becoming one of the first legal slaveholders in the colonies.

Genevieve Belly Ricard of Louisiana belonged to a small band of *gens de couleur libres* who bought and sold large quantities of land, sugar, rice, cotton, livestock, machinery, and slaves. When her husband, Cyprian Ricard, died, she inherited his thriving plantation; thereafter, the widow Ricard, as she was known, successfully managed (with the help but not the supervision of her son), about a thousand acres and close to a hundred slaves, valued at $200,000 on the eve of the Civil War.

More modestly, Negroland citizens are ministers, teachers, and skilled artisans. They own property that they rent out; they own inns and modest hotels; they are barbers, carpenters, mechanics, tailors, jewelers, bakers, and dressmakers. The majority are of mixed racial ancestry because that ancestry gives them more access to well-placed white patrons and relatives.

What did it mean to be a privileged free Negro? It meant you were free to earn money; free to marry legally and (sometimes) showily; free to educate your legally free children and pass property on to them; free to travel, to buy a summer home; free to form reading societies, debating societies, mutual aid societies; free, if you were a female, to cultivate "the lighter accomplishments . . . to show much taste and skill in painting, instrumental music, singing and the various departments of ornamental needlework &c."; free to hire a maid and a nanny; free to have your own version of the Social Register.

Free in the North to agitate against slavery and for voting rights while excluding Negroes with fewer accomplishments from your social circles.

Free in the South to lobby for your fluctuating rights while deeming it wise to ignore the claims of poorer, darker free Negroes.

Free to labor for privilege in the hopes that your children would be entitled to it.

"You have seen how a man was made a slave; now you shall see how a slave was made a man," wrote Frederick Douglass in his autobiography. Let us see how slaves, male and female, become social arbiters and leaders. One Negro elite to declare itself in print and begin publishing its stories in the early nineteenth century was comprised of escaped slaves like Douglass, like William Wells Brown, like Ellen and William Craft.

Even the first author to formally define "the elite of our people" had, in his quiet way, escaped slavery. In 1841 Joseph Willson, dentist, of Philadelphia, published *Sketches of the Higher Classes of Colored Society*. He used the pseudonym "A Southerner." He was born Joseph Keating in Augusta, Georgia, first son of a wealthy middle-aged slaveholder, John Willson Jr., unmarried, and a teenage slave, Betsy Keating, unmarried and freed by Willson before she bore the first of their five children. The couple had a pedigree of sorts: for many years, Betsy's slave aunt had served John's slaveholding uncle. His will declared her, their daughter, and her siblings free, "on account of her care and attention to my domestic concerns." Ah, the clinical euphemisms of the law.

Joseph was just five when his father died in 1822. The will provided the Negro family with shares in the Augusta bank Willson had helped found, as well as the protection of a trustworthy executor and a rent-free house in the country, with "suitable household and Kitchen furniture and an adequate number of male and female Servants to wait upon them." Were all those servants slaves? Had Betsy known any of them in her youth?

She had begun her life as a slave wench; she became an astute and planful matron. The Keatings lived in discreet comfort for eleven years. As formal education for Negroes was forbidden in Georgia, she sent her sons out of state for schooling and had her daughters tutored at home. Each year the state looked with increasing disfavor on free persons of color and found new ways to limit their actions and opportunities. In 1833, when Joseph was sixteen, Georgia marshaled its resources to pass laws that (1) fined any person who allowed a slave or free Negro access to a printing press or any other labor requiring a knowledge of reading and writing; (2) forbade any person to teach a slave or

free Negro to read or write; and (3) allowed a free Negro con-
victed of "living an idle life" (which could mean walking down
the street at a leisurely pace) to be sold into slavery. The family relocated to Philadelphia, long known for its community of
achieving Negroes.

Betsy Keating was wise in the ways of social discretion. In Philadelphia she became Mrs. Elizabeth Willson, widow. She bought
a three-story house in a largely white neighborhood—she knew
how to live quietly among white people—then joined the prestigious St. Thomas's African Episcopal Church and set about
introducing her family to Negro society. They were attractive,
and they formed solid ties in that small, watchful world. Joseph
found a mentor in another Southern Negro émigré, Frederick
Augustus Hinton, who was a fervent abolitionist as well as a
barber and perfumer to the city's white elite. Hinton arranged
for Joseph to learn that once-forbidden printer's trade—not in
Philadelphia, where custom encouraged white printers to deny
Negroes training, but in Boston, under the fervent white abolitionist William Lloyd Garrison. When Joseph returned to Philadelphia, he opened a printing business and married a young
lady from Georgia of like background. Elizabeth Harnett was
the daughter of a Scottish slaveholder and a free woman of color.

What a relief it must have been for this young couple to talk
together openly about their parents and their histories!

Willson's book sets the tone for another 150 years of prose on
the subject. The very idea of "Higher Classes" of colored society
will "undoubtedly excite the mirth of a prejudiced community
on its annunciation," he declares; nevertheless, "it is perfectly
correct and proper." He aims to "remove" the unfounded and

widespread prejudice of the white reader. He also aims to correct the tonal abuse of English writers like Frederick Marryat, Harriet Martineau, and Frances Trollope, who had skewered American customs and manners to great acclaim. By so doing he demonstrates that he is perfectly capable of passing literary and ethical judgments on the white world. And though he does intend to address certain behavioral "abuses" of colored society, he assures his people that they will "discover none but the best of feelings throughout has had any influence in guiding the pen of their humble servant, The Author."

He is clearly on the defensive, as generations of future chroniclers will be. "The prejudiced world has for a long time been in error in judging of what may be termed *the home condition,* or social intercourse, of the higher classes of colored society by the specimens who in the everyday walks of life are presented to their view as 'the hewers of wood and the drawers of water.' This rash mode of judgment—the forming of an opinion of the beauty of the landscape by the heavy shading in the fore-ground of the picture—has been the source of many groundless and unjust aspersions against their general character, and one which common justice requires should be removed."

To establish his intellectual acumen, Willson lists the usual criteria for defining elites—wealth, education, occupation, birth, family connections—then qualifies them. The higher class, according to him, is "that portion of colored society whose incomes, from their pursuits or otherwise (immoralities or criminalities of course excepted), enables them to maintain the position of house-holders and their families in relative ease and comfort." Further, their incomes allow them, and their instincts encourage them, to pursue education, acquire culture, and embrace moral causes from temperance to abolitionism. He is determined to avoid boasts, grandiosity. He is determined to set high standards, to question (if a touch rhetorically) the worth of any distinction not founded chiefly on virtue. He respects upward mobility that displays itself as self-improvement. He deplores the petty social feuds and rivalries that hinder the work of racial advancement.

Is it any surprise that he writes formal, rather eighteenth-century prose, quoting Shakespeare, Alexander Pope, and Thomas Gray, or that he savors highly constructed metaphors and diction?

> The machinery of the watch will not fulfill its intent, unless the impulse of the spring be applied; and, though things inanimate are not to be compared with the human soul, yet, neither can a man be expected to rise to eminence in a given department, where, as is the case with men of color, there is not only an absence of all encouragement—all impulse—all definite motive to cheer him onward—but from the exercise of the legitimate functions of which, even were he fitted therefor, he would be absolutely excluded!

There are no reports on his speaking voice, but surely all evidence of a Southern accent had been eradicated. I'm moved by his choice of image: the tension between a perfectly constructed mechanism and a human soul striving to function perfectly, because of course the human can never attain that kind of perfection, any more than a Negro in antebellum America could be accorded perfect respect or equality.

Why did he choose the pseudonym "A Southerner"? His authorship was well known to the colored elite he wrote of. Still, it offered an appearance of discretion he must have hoped would calm their fear that any public criticism might inflame Anglo-

Saxon prejudice. At moments he seems to imply that only "A Southerner" knows just how fragile Negro rights are, even in the North. Pennsylvania Negroes would do well, he counsels, to pursue their interests "in the manner of suitors; and show themselves very humble in the exercise of even that prerogative."

He may have hoped his moniker would encourage Northern white readers to think themselves liberal compared to Southern slaveholders, and give more credence to his observations. In fact, after receiving a small number of respectable reviews in both white and Negro newspapers, the book disappeared. White reviewers amiably condescended. One, an abolitionist, "glanced" at the work to find that "its outward appearance seems creditable," and that the author, "himself a colored man," showed some writing ability. Another lauded Willson for correcting his people's "errors," but failed to notice that he was far more eager to correct white people. Negro reviewers took pains to show their insider knowledge: one recorded the "disapprobation" of certain members of the higher classes; another commended the author's "moral courage," given the subject's delicacy. Already we were keeping close count of our achievements: written in "rather good style" (a touch of fraternal competition here?), Willson's book, noted the reviewer, "adds to the number of our authors."

Almost twenty years later—two years before the Civil War—author Cyprian Clamorgan publishes *The Colored Aristocracy of St. Louis*. He offers a much showier, more worldly view. The times have changed and, in keeping with his florid, luxuriant name, he savors certain tonal liberties.

Clamorgan opens by making clear that he is a man on intimate terms with all kinds of important people, from "Fred. Douglass and his able compatriots" to eighteenth-century voyageur-grandees like his grandfather, who was among the First White Families of St. Louis. In their travels, Clamorgan explains, such men, while trading in land, fur, and slaves, sometimes "obtained wives" with the blood of Africa in their veins, and from this commingling came the colored aristocracy of the city: "those who move in a certain circle; who, by means of wealth, education, or natural ability, form a peculiar class—the elite of the colored race." His grandfather obtained and owned a series of such wives, owning all and marrying none; his grandmother was the third of five who bore the grandee's children. The colored Clamorgans inherited property from this grandee, who, they claimed, had been awarded about a half million acres by the king of Spain in 1796.

Cyprian belongs to what he jauntily calls the "tonsorial profession." Starting out as a barber in one of the city's fine hotels, he then entered business with his brothers, who owned a "Depot of Elegant French and English Parfumeries, Toilet and Fancy Articles, Combs, Brushes, Razors &c." Many colored aristocrats are "knights of the razor"—could it be, he posits, that they are the only men in the community who truly enjoy free speech? After all, "they take the white man by the nose without giving offense and without causing an effusion of blood." He likes his little jests.

Cyprian flaunts his birth and skin color as well as his people's looks, money, property, and fine taste; he considers himself more arbiter than chronicler. Joseph Willson would have shuddered to name a gentleman's income, speak of a lady's amours, or salute those "separated from the white race by a line of division so faint that it can be traced only by the keen eye of prejudice." But we have left the East for a city where brash Western manners meet Southern extravagance; where blood is hot; where fortunes and reputations are made and squandered every day.

So the book is arranged like a tour of the great houses, part boosterism, part scandal sheet.

"If the reader will accompany me down Seventh street to the vicinity of Rutgers, I will show him a large mansion, which, with the yard and out-buildings, occupies half a block of ground. Entering this mansion, I will introduce him to its mistress." That would have been Mrs. Pelagie Rutgers, a former slave who purchased her freedom for three dollars and is now worth half a million: "Mrs. Rutgers is an illiterate woman, but lives in good style; she has in her house a piano which cost two thousand dollars but her wealthy daughter, the sole heiress to her large estate, is not able to play upon it." Dashing Samuel Mordecai made his fortune in gambling, "and is good for one hundred thousand dollars when flush"; his daughter was sent to England for her schooling, and he talks of settling in Paris, where "he would be received into the first circles."

William Johnson opened a barbershop, set money aside, bought a city block for $1,000 when real estate values were low, then sold it for $100,000: "Not so bad a speculation for a colored man!" Cyprian commends ladies for their intelligence but dwells far more on the particulars of their skin tone, hair grade, and social graces or lapses.

London Berry "is a good man, his only fault being too great a fondness for cards." Recently, though, his wife committed the faux pas of attending a ball given by the "second class of colored people" and has been banned from the better parties ever since. Cyprian's judicious counsel: "They are both no doubt sorry for their conduct and will be again received next winter and their indiscretion forgiven."

The "rather dilapidated" Mrs. Pelagie Foreman, he notes with spiteful satisfaction, was once a fascinating but saucy "lump of yellow flesh" who earned a cowhiding she probably deserved from her white lover; her indiscretions have made her a social outcast, but (this he notes with approval) she remains a shrewd property owner who "can command the cool sum of one hundred thousand dollars."

Other cities, North and South, have their variously flavored antebellum elites: among the most established are in Boston, New York, Baltimore, Washington, D.C., Atlanta, Lexington, Fayetteville, Natchez, Cincinnati, and Cleveland. Sociologically, they range from petit bourgeois to lower upper class and middle upper class. Their ancestries, as they are always proud to boast, extend into the highest ranks of white society. Strains of Indian and African royalty are also welcome.

Cyprian Clamorgan ends his *Colored Aristocracy* with a promise to write a second book about the "second" class of colored St. Louisians—those who give balls the aristocrats are expected not to attend, and whose exploits "will startle many of our white friends." But it is 1858. He had begun his book by invoking Harriet Beecher Stowe, Solomon Northrup, and Frederick Douglass; he had declared Missouri's Emancipation Party "the result of the unwearied and combined action of the wealthy free colored men of St. Louis, who know that the abolition of slavery in Missouri would remove a stigma from their race, and elevate them in the scale of society." His second book never appeared. It was the Civil War that elevated the wealthy, the poor, the free, and the enslaved colored men, women, and children.

1861–1865: In the South male slaves build Confederate forts, make Confederate artillery, maintain Confederate railroads, serve their masters in Confederate army camps. Women slaves work the fields that produce food for the Confederate army, cook and clean for Confederate mistresses who now run farms and plantations in the absence of their men, care for the children of those Confederate mistresses, care for their own children, cook and clean, and nurse soldiers in Confederate hospitals. As the war goes on, slaves begin to desert their owners, flee Confederate fields and towns for Union army camps, where—as contraband rather than slave property—the men build forts, repair railroads, haul supplies and equipment, and serve as scouts and spies for Union troops, while the women cook and clean in the camps, nurse soldiers, serve as scouts and spies for Union troops, and take care of the children they have brought along.

Free Negroes struggle to defeat or evade new laws that constrict their liberties. A small mulatto upper class swears loyalty to the Southern cause and volunteers to fight for it. (Nearly all such offers are refused: equality of sword and musket is not an appealing notion to the Confederate army.) Negroes who own land and slaves are expected to use both to provide food and labor for the Confederate troops. Others, less conspicuous, lie low, even do what they can to aid the cause of freedom: prepare themselves to be leaders when the war ends and slavery is past and gone, when they have a Negro community and constituency to lead.

Free Negroes who emigrated north shortly before the war have learned the inconvenient truths that Northern Negroes have long known: many public accommodations are closed to them; most churches are closed to them; most schools are closed to their children. Law and custom restrict their right to use the job skills they have or to acquire new ones: white workers do not want them as competition.

Two years into a war the Union fears losing, the Emancipation Proclamation frees the slaves. Negro men are at last permitted to enlist in the Union army. Approximately 180,000, North and South, do so. It's a chance for them to prove their competence and their loyalty; it's a new job market, even if for most of the war they are paid less than their white counterparts. War gives Negro women new jobs too, or at least new settings for old jobs. Most of them still cook, clean, launder, sew, and nurse: now they cook, clean, launder, sew, and nurse for their country, in Union hospitals and camps. They are paid less, for the war's duration, than their white counterparts.

Still, there are life-changing opportunities for a small group of free Negroes who claim membership in the higher ranks of the abolitionist movement. Some have been free for years; they're leaders in their communities. Some are the former slaves who've won national recognition by publishing narratives of their lives. These men and women travel America and Europe to lecture on the evils of slavery, to urge immediate emancipation, to collect funds for war relief. A few even travel south to teach eager, provisionally freed slaves (Union army contrabands) to read and write. A life-changing opportunity and a profound culture shock.

October 1862: Charlotte Forten arrives in South Carolina. She is from one of Philadelphia's most distinguished colored families, prominent abolitionists since the eighteenth century (James Forten was her grandfather). She was the first of her race to graduate from the Salem Normal School of Salem, Massachusetts, and she has come to Port Royal to teach reading and writing to the contraband slaves freed by the Union army. "On the wharf was a motley assemblage—soldiers, officers and 'contrabands' of every hue and size. They were mostly black, however, and certainly the most dismal specimens I ever saw," she tells her journal. Later that night, waiting in the commissary's office, she encounters the "the little Commissary himself, . . . a perfect little popinjay, and he and a Colonel somebody who didn't look any too sensible, talked in a very smart manner, evidently for our especial benefit. The word 'nigger' was plentifully used, whereupon I set them down at once as *not* gentlemen."

She is twenty-five years old and has spent her life studying French and Latin, astronomy and history; reading Spenser, Milton, and Elizabeth Barrett Browning; Dickens, the Brontës, Emerson, and Stowe; *The Atlantic* and *The Liberator*. She has socialized with renowned abolitionists, colored and white; she faithfully attends literary lectures and antislavery meetings; she always disparages the occasional poem or essay she contributes to antislavery journals.

She rages against bigotries, big and small; falls into a depression ("I wonder that every colored person is not a misanthrope. Surely we have everything to make us hate mankind"), then upbraids herself for being insufficiently stoic. She strives for perfect selflessness. "Conscience answers it is wrong, it is ignoble to despair . . . Let us take courage, never ceasing to work,—hoping and believing that if not for us, for another generation there is a better, brighter day in store." She sinks back into self-doubt. She is not a misanthrope, she is a melancholic—a depressed gentle-woman.

Dutifully, doggedly, she teaches at a white elementary school in Massachusetts and a black elementary school in Philadelphia before ill health threatens her ability to earn her living. She longs to visit Italy; she longs to be a literary genius, to do something that will make her "forever known." She doubts her abilities and opportunities. She resolves: "I will pray that God, in his goodness, will make me noble enough to find my highest happiness in doing my duty."

It's so easy, so temptingly easy, to upbraid or at least mock her pieties, the decorum that dulls her, the taint of naïve snobbery. How pleased and surprised she is that some of her students are so very bright; how laughable she finds their ebullience and physical intensity. (The leader of the singers one Sunday is Prince, large, black, and "full of the shouting spirit . . . It was amusing to see his gymnastic performances. They were quite in the Ethiopian Methodists' style.")

"These people have really a great deal of musical talent," she writes in a letter to *The Liberator,* adding, as so many white listeners have and will, that their songs are nearly impossible to describe: "They are so wild, so strange, and yet so invariably harmonious and sweet." How she basks in the courtesies of Thomas Wentworth Higginson and Colonel Robert Shaw! Yet how could it be otherwise? Progressive white easterners have been part of her world since childhood; contraband slaves and working-class Negroes have not. And free Negroes have had to depend on the decency of progressives. We know that slaves made distinctions between good and bad white people and behaved accordingly. Free Negroes did the same. In both cases there can be a display of gratitude (excited, fawning, a touch abject) that makes us wince.

Nevertheless, Charlotte Forten does establish genuine relations with some of the blacks in Port Royal. And when Higginson's black regiment prepares to go to Jacksonville, Florida, she is invited along as their teacher. (The town's evacuation prevents the trip.) Poor lungs, blinding headaches, and loneliness—what she later calls fears of insanity—send her home after eighteen months. There, filled with self-reproach, she works for organizations that educate New England's freedmen and freedwomen. She aspires to "that noblest of compensations," as she writes a friend: "the knowledge that you are giving your life to the regeneration of a down-trodden & long suffering people."

The war ends; "Reconstruction" begins. Rights are asserted, granted, withdrawn; demanded, restored, amended. Opportunities are sought and fought for; bestowed and withheld. A constitutional amendment forbids slavery. Southern blacks farm their own land, start businesses, and venture into new professions; open more schools and churches, seek education in long-established white schools and newly founded black schools; demand better wages, win political representation in state and federal governments.

And, right from the beginning, Southern states use legal and illegal means (laws, sporadic violence, organized terrorism) to thwart wage increases and fair employment practices; to force Negroes back into a plantation labor system that will be called sharecropping; to limit or deny political advancement to Negro men, women, and children; to limit or deny education to Negro men, women, and children. Every advance is met with an attack.

> 1865 and '66: Pass a civil rights act; found the Ku Klux
> Klan.
> 1868: The Fourteenth Amendment grants Negro men the
> vote. The Fourteenth Amendment denies all women—
> Negro, white, and other—the vote. Five years later, the
> Fifteenth Amendment prohibits state governments from
> finding ways to deprive citizens of the right to vote based
> on race. The Fifteenth Amendment does not protect
> the rights of blacks to hold office. Nor does it prevent
> Southern states from launching their assault and battery
> on these constitutional rights with a flurry of laws called
> the Black Codes and a series of terrorist attacks by
> the KKK.

Despite all this, Negroes are acquiring political resources and limited amounts of political and social power. In the decades after the war, free Negroes who had privilege before the war and Negroes who were in the top tier of slavery acquire power as politicians and community leaders. They work to balance their continued and expanding social privilege with their equally expanded duties to the larger Negro community.

But there are new players here. Those who once lived in slavery or on the lower rungs of the free Negro class are now in a position to seize opportunities and provide good schools, stores, and restaurants to an eager people along with churches, life insurance, good hair products, and cultural advantages. They too become teachers, lawyers, undertakers, doctors, journalists;

some dare to become artists. They study chemistry and zoology, Greek, Latin, the Romance languages. They send their children to the growing number of Negro colleges; occasionally they send them to white colleges; periodically they send them abroad for cultural enrichment.

The old families have to cope: The end of slavery has not just freed a people; it has freed achievers, strivers, arrivistes from the lower ranks. Call them what you will. That many have darker skin is often noted by the old elites; likewise their rough manners and rowdy ways. Their homes and wardrobes are said to be gaudy, their voices have a telltale Southern timbre; their grammar can be . . . deviant. But they are here. They will achieve and advance; they will buy or barter their way into the old elite; they will establish their own vigorous competing elite.

What has become of those old aristocrats Joseph Willson, Cyprian Clamorgan, and Charlotte Forten?

Joseph Willson has flourished. He is Dr. Willson now, dental surgeon. In the 1850s he moved his family to Cleveland, which boasted a Negro elite as secure as Philadelphia's. His practice thrives; his patients are respectable Negroes and Caucasians; Joseph's wife, Elizabeth, is known as a fine musician and gracious hostess. They join a prestigious, largely white Episcopal church, and a club whose aim is "to promote social intercourse and cultural contact among the better educated colored families" of the city. Their son becomes a lawyer, their daughters become schoolteachers (a typical gender division for that and many subsequent generations). In 1878 the youngest daughter achieves something her paternal slave grandmother never could have: a fine, fashionable marriage to a powerful Southern gentleman. Blanche K. Bruce, her new husband, is a mulatto ex-slave who grew up to be a teacher, then the owner of a 640-acre plantation, and finally a senator from the Magnolia State of Mississippi.

Cyprian Clamorgan has done less well. He has had two disappointing marriages. His first wife, Joanna, died; and after a few years he sees very little of the second, Hebe, or their daughter, Mary. Since the war's end he has worked on boats as a barber and a steward, moving among St. Louis, New Orleans, and Calhoun County, Illinois. When it's to his advantage, he passes for white. (He spent the war in New Orleans, race and profession unknown.) When his money runs short, he sells off some of the tracts of the land he and his relatives inherited from their grandee grandfather. Much of it is no longer in Clamorgan hands: time and again—in the 1860s, the 1870s, the 1880s and '90s—the family sues the railroad companies and the individuals who now occupy their land. Time and again they lose.

Charlotte Forten has continued to work for "a downtrodden & long suffering people," arranging Northern support for teachers in the South, and briefly returning South to teach. She moves to Washington, D.C., to teach in the Preparatory High School for Colored Youth that will become Dunbar High, renowned for educating future race leaders and ornaments. She works as a clerk for the U.S. Treasury. She marries the minister and race leader Francis Grimké in 1878, and spends the rest of her life as a physically frail, unswervingly diligent writer, activist, and helpmate.

These are years of ferocious industrial and technological growth: steel, iron, railroads, electricity. Of ferocious social strife: monopolies vs. labor unions; political machines vs. civic reformers; immigrants vs. nativists; economic booms and crashes; new millionaires vs. old ones; an expanding middle class vs. ever-growing numbers of the poor and the almost-poor. Whites instigate riots, South and North, and lynchings, usually South; whites pass federal and state laws that ensure exclusion of or inferior accommodation for blacks in every kind of public activity and space: train and bus travel, hospitals, restaurants, libraries, theaters, parks, beaches, and schools, from the nursery to the university.

How do our chroniclers address this?

Our female chroniclers cannot address any of it without addressing rape and miscegenation. First they must defend their long-debased reputation as Negro women, deemed inherently lascivious since slave times, incapable of being virtuous wives and mothers. Second, they must protest the growing number of lynchings, most of them based on postslavery claims that Negro men were compulsive rapists of white women.

In 1895 Ida B. Wells, a young schoolteacher turned journalist, the daughter of emancipated slaves determined to advance by educating themselves and their children, publishes *The Red Record: Tabulated Statistics and Alleged Causes of Lynching in the United States.* The "record" includes the lynching of Negroes "for almost any offense from murder to a misdemeanor"; the lynching of men, women, and children charged with rioting or insurrection; the lynching of Negroes whose political or economic success threatens whites; the lynching of Negro men who have been having consensual affairs with white women.

She collects her evidence from white newspapers and legal documents as well as from Negro witnesses and newspapers. She presents it in crisp, vivid, spicy anecdotes, followed by zealous argument.

The Southern white man says that it is impossible for a voluntary alliance to exist between a white woman and a col-

ored man, and therefore, the fact of an alliance is a proof of
force. In numerous instances where colored men have been
lynched on the charge of rape, it was positively known at the
time of lynching, and indisputably proven after the victim's
death, that the relationship sustained between the man and
woman was voluntary and clandestine, and that in no court
of law could even the charge of assault have been successfully maintained.

As for legions of lascivious colored women, "The miscegenation laws of the South only operate against the legitimate union
of the races, they leave the white man free to seduce all the
colored girls he can,—and, [here she provides documented evi-
dence] to rape them as well."

A Voice from the South, by "A Black Woman of the South,"
has appeared in 1892. The black woman behind the pen name
is Anna Julia Cooper, daughter of a slave master and a slave
woman; educated at Oberlin (with no help from her father);
a teacher of math, science, and Latin at Washington, D.C.'s
respected Preparatory High School for Colored Youth.

Her prose is that of a self-contained and rigorously cultivated
Victorian, filled with literary allusions, historical comparisons,
and Christian invocations. She excoriates the "masculinist" urge
to dominate, first in the home, then in the nation and throughout the world.

The pen name shows her wish to invoke the collective voice of
an unheeded, uncelebrated female Anonymous, a black Anonymous who speaks to and for all of the oppressed. Woman's cause
is—or should be—"linked with that of every agony that has
been dumb—every wrong that needs a voice."

Like so many women's rights leaders, she insists on believing
women possess sympathies and spiritual gifts men lack. But—

and here she becomes a tough-minded political pragmatist—
women cannot reform society without working to educate
themselves. And white women can reform nothing until and
unless they are willing to relinquish their caste privilege, those
codes of racial and social superiority they extol in their men and
instill in their children.

Nevertheless, she is filled with hope: "such new and alluring
vistas are opening out before us, such original and radical sug-
gestions for the adjustment of labor and capital, of government
and the governed, of the family, the church and the state." She
exults: "To be a woman in such an age carries with it privilege
and an opportunity never implied before. But to be a woman
of the Negro race in America, and to be able to grasp the deep
significance of the possibilities of the crisis, is to have a heritage,
it seems to me, unique in the ages."

And this sense of destiny galvanizes a critical mass of privileged Negro women. Few are willing to call themselves black,
as Cooper did; few are as militantly forthright as Wells. Many
insist overmuch that they be recognized as *ladies*. Proud of their
education and cultivation, they are angered and ashamed to be
classed with "the lowly, the illiterate and even the vicious, to
whom they are bound by the ties of race and sex." But they go
to work. They set about to reclaim and redeem these women,
and in doing so to uplift the race. They form clubs and associations to raise money for schools and settlement houses; organize
nurseries and kindergartens; teach reading, writing, sewing,
homemaking, and hygiene; work for women's suffrage, for temperance, for better work conditions, and for anti-lynching laws.
When they form a National Association of Colored Women's
Clubs, they choose as their motto "Lifting As We Climb." Ardu-
ous. Virtuous. High-minded and high-handed.

The twentieth century beckons. In 1903 the high-minded, high-handed New Englander W. E. B. Du Bois publishes *The Souls of Black Folk,* in which he joins scholarship, reflection, exhortation, and confession. He is a Victorian, but he is a modernist too. Stern and stringent. And he is proud: "Does any race produce more than a small percentage of exceptional men and women—ten percent at most?" he demands in another essay published that same year. "Is any nation civilized from the bottom up?" The demure exclusivity of Willson's "colored elite" is now the more sociologically rigorous, politically aggressive "Talented Tenth," from whose ranks race leaders must come. Clamorgan's gleeful frivolity has been altogether banished. Cooper's Christianity is not a deeply held faith; it's a moral trope, a way for Du Bois to invoke the eternal verities of justice and injustice.

He shares Cooper's radical romanticism; he shares Wells's outrage at lynchings and other Southern barbarities. He knows their work.

But he is intent on cutting a much wider swath, sometimes at their expense. The soul of a grandly confident Negro intellectual—a Negro *male* intellectual—is on display. Du Bois is blazingly entitled. And Du Bois sets the agenda for generations to come: The educated and privileged must guide the Mass of Negroes forward, fight oppression, and champion achievement. Unlike its predecessors, *The Souls of Black Folk* excites intellectual debate and stirs serious readers on both sides of the increasingly rigid color line. James Weldon Johnson compares its impact to that of *Uncle Tom's Cabin;* Henry James calls it "the only Southern book of any real distinction to appear in years"—and laments the fact that a depleted white Southern culture has made it so. His reaction illustrates another crucial Du Boisian theme. Men and women of the Talented Tenth may cherish Shakespeare, Dumas, and Balzac (or Henry James) all they want, but they know that in the hearts and minds of most Americans they are unwelcome pretenders trying to escape their rightful place in the lower social and biological order. That is the double consciousness they must bear. Or one form of it. The other is the double consciousness that comes from knowing history has bound them to cruelties and calumnies that many hours of the day, many days of the week, many weeks of the year they feel or want to feel little attachment to. *No,* they tell themselves then, *I have worked to earn the right to go about the business of my well-appointed life—to fulfill my professional obligations, social aspirations, familial responsibilities. I do not want to think constantly about Them as Us.*

In 1948 Du Bois will offer a stern, stringent critique of the Talented Tenth to a proud organization of its leading professional men. Invoking Marx to the members of the Boulé, he will urge on them "a willingness to sacrifice and plan for . . . economic revolution in industry and a just distribution of wealth." He had always known, he said, that a Talented Tenth might become no more than "a group of selfish, self-indulgent, well-to-do men whose basic interest in solving the Negro problem was personal; personal freedom and use of the world" with no "arousing care as to what became of the mass of American Negroes."

Nine years later a black Marxist and sociologist Du Bois has mentored will turn his challenge into verbal cudgels.

It is 1957, and Chicago sociologist E. Franklin Frazier has published *Black Bourgeoisie.* The title says it all. Despite its longings, the Talented Tenth is still black, and for all its class pretensions, it is merely bourgeois. Its members have scant financial or political power, so they delude themselves with compensatory boasts and rivalries. They have abandoned their role as responsible race leaders and exemplars; they disdain the masses and avoid them as much as possible.

They are strivers, not aristocrats; arrivistes with no real point of arrival. Their inferiority complex shows itself in a "pathological struggle for status within the Negro world and craving for recognition in the white world." Double consciousness has been reduced to imitation and compensation.

Frazier refuses the role of traitor. Instead, his subjects' shock and anger fuels his confidence. As he will later note with dry satisfaction, "It appears that middle-class Negroes were able to see themselves for the first time and, as they feared, in the way they appeared to outsiders."

It wasn't pretty.

Nevertheless, we of Negroland played our part in the civil rights movement that was unfurling and erupting. We were in the courts, in the press, on the streets and freedom buses; we were leaders, followers, and financial supporters. By the late sixties, leftist politics and cultural nationalism had given the once-shunned nomenclature "black" a deep and lustrous sheen. Black Power, Black Beauty, Black Studies, the Black Man and (as bulwark and adornment) the Black Woman. We adapted, with some internal dissent. And we profited.

In the 1970s white society scurries to include us in its ranks. We become mayors and members of Congress; journalists at white periodicals and TV stations; partners or at least entry-level lawyers at white firms; we trade bonds on Wall Street; we work at corporations (usually as directors of human resources).

But now a tide of political conservatism is rising. Likewise a marketable form of ethnic pride is being conceived. One result is a series of up-with-aristocracy books and articles about minority groups. A prolific writer of Anglo-Saxon ancestry named Stephen Birmingham leads the charge with *Our Crowd: The Great Jewish Families of New York* (1967), *Real Lace: America's Irish Rich* (1973), and *Certain People: America's Black Elite* (1977, with a mahogany-brown cover, no less). Certain of his subjects find his sources questionable and his tone familiar.

Fortunately, a year before, one of our own, a longtime black society columnist, produces a bicentennial coffee table book celebrating our history from the seventeenth to the late twentieth century. It is a gold-colored book. It is *Black Society* by Gerri Major: "I have lived it for over eighty years," she proclaims, "and before me my family lived it." (For decades she chronicled its doings in black magazines and newspapers.) Her declaration of independence? "The miscegenated family tree has been supplanted by stocks, bonds, bank accounts, real estate and/or high professional standing. All proudly proclaiming their Black identity." They are not chimerical and they are not anachronistic.

Major's book is read almost exclusively by the black society she writes of. It is celebratory but not grandiose—a pleasing bicentennial artifact.

The twentieth century has just one year left when an insider's account of black society finds a mainstream white publisher and attracts white media attention that verges on excitement. If Major was a chatty chronicler, Lawrence Otis Graham is a sprightly gossip in the Clamorgan mode: he writes largely for white magazines and is considered something of an upstart by old-line blacks. His 1999 *Our Kind of People: Inside America's Black Upper Class* is a cross-country social whirl of interviews and personal anecdotes. Graham chronicles our old ways, and makes sure to certify their current value with the status symbols of integration; "exclusive" and "prestigious" schools and neighborhoods; "impeccable," even "inspiring" professional credentials; friendships and alliances with "the WASP elite" and "top celebrities."

But I belong to an earlier generation, that of the fifties and sixties: it's us and our predecessors I want to write of. Most whites knew little about us; only a few cared to know. We were taught that we embodied the best that was known and thought in— and of—Negro life. We were taught to resent the relative lack of attention our achievements garnered. We were taught that we were better than the whites who looked down on us—that we were better than most whites, period. But that this would rarely if ever be acknowledged by white people, with all their entitlement. Not the entitlement a government provides, but the kind history bestows. This is your birthright, says history.

Privilege is provisional. Privilege can be denied, withheld, offered grudgingly and summarily withdrawn. Entitlement is impervious to the kinds of verbs that modify privilege. Our people have had to work, scrape for privilege, gobble it down when those who would snatch it away weren't looking.

Keep a close watch.

March 6, 1944, Tombstone, Arizona

My mother had joined my father at Fort Huachuca, Arizona, where many Negro units were stationed during the war. The army was still segregated, so all facilities, from civilian quarters to hospitals, were built in duplicate. One for white army personnel, one for Negro.

The base hospital where my father served was the largest Negro hospital in the United States and the only one in the army to be staffed and commanded by Negroes. This relative independence did not hold elsewhere in the military. As Chicagoan Welton Taylor* writes in his memoir, Two Steps from Glory: A World War II Liaison Pilot Confronts Jim Crow and the Enemy in the South Pacific: *"Virtually all Negro field artillery officers, including those sent to Fort Huachuca, were forced to serve under white senior officers and battery commanders. The Army kept Negroes 'in their place' no matter where they were."*

My father's rank was captain. The Fort Huachuca hospital staff included friends of his from Provident Hospital in Chicago. On March 6, 1944, my mother was three months pregnant with my sister, Denise. This is what she wrote to Deborah Joseph Raines, her dear friend from Delta and the University of Chicago:

---

* Welton Taylor is a research microbiologist. He taught at the medical schools of the University of Illinois and Northwestern.

Dearest Debbie,

The process of your domestication sounds wonderful. I don't half mind mine either. Since I've been out here, cooking and fluffing up his pillows, Ronald's gotten rather Taftish*—and he, as poor as the snake who didn't have a pit to hiss in! (Did I say something)?

A clerical job is not for his wife. Red Cross would be OK, but I've worked hard enough and will have to scuffle again soon enough, so that I should gather ye rosebuds while I may (his remarks). Despite your earlier efforts to send me here, I'm glad I stayed as long as I did or we wouldn't have a thing to show for being married but love, and we've got that anyway. Altho' I've bought nothing for myself, and there's nothing to spend money for other than just living, that's so high.

However I'm glad I'm here at this time, which has been the worst time for my little playmate. Surprisingly enough, he is doing very well, for which I flatter myself and my presence . . .

You know, of course, that this past week we've been congratulating three Lt. Col's and a full Col.—all well deserved. I'm just mad that we didn't get in on the political-move-gravy train. Nothing for the lower-ranking officers . . .

We had a letter from Joe Mitchell (P.H., x-ray) in Australia.† His wife is back in Los Angeles with her family and working in the P.O. Sparky Matthews' family is visiting him and are temporarily next door.‡ It's a relief to talk with someone who hasn't been beaten down to the narrowness of most of the gals here. Tombstone now boasts thirteen Negro

---

* Taft C. Raines was a surgeon on the staff at Provident Hospital. He was round and full to my father's thin and bony.
† Joseph Mitchell was a radiologist at Provident.
‡ Henry "Sparky" Matthews was an internist at Provident. His wife, Harryetta Matthews, became one of my mother's best friends.

families. We hear a couple of malcontents have begun to fret over the "Negro Problem of Tombstone," probably because we're all obviously used to more than any of them—else they wouldn't be here.

We play pennyante, rotating houses each Sat. night, and Ronald and I are $12 ahead. In the barracks morale is so low and work so scarce that thousands pass hands in a month. One fellow has made $2500 in poker and blackjack in two months. Of course, there are smaller games in the barracks too. Last I heard, Shaw* was dealing deuces wild . . .

Saw *The Uninvited* last night and enjoyed it very much. No suggestion of war, and tho' the plot is impossible it's so well done that it keeps you with the tenseness you had at *Rebecca* and *Wuthering Heights*. Saw also *Jane Eyre* and didn't mind Orson Welles at all as the critics did. Luther Adler, to me, brought the same storminess and moodiness to the role. It's different in parts from the play tho'. Also, Lena's latest where she does "Brazilian Boogie," is nice. Didn't like one of her outfits, nor Hazel Scott's . . .

Did our little girl Frances something make the Pyramid Club? I hear Richardson† is supposed to be engaged after a fashion. Is it Florence Jace?‡ I understand he was rather fond of her.

I hear also in these parts that the Horace Caytons may be divorced, but no one has nerve enough to ask for a statement for the grapevine press. And he's supposed to be squiring Delores Renfroe and Florence Draper.§

---

* Maurice Shaw was an ob-gyn at Provident.
† James Richardson was an ophthalmologist on staff at Provident.
‡ A Delta pledgee, my mother thinks.
§ Horace Cayton was a sociologist. *Black Metropolis,* which he co-authored with St. Clair Drake, would be published the next year. His wife—they married and divorced twice—

Ole Ronald is 160&½ pounds of fineness now and I am still fighting avoirdupois. I think we're both quite glad we're married to each other. Tell Hertha[*] I wish her all the happiness I have, 'cause that's as much as anyone could wish. Sometimes I almost forget I'm a Negro. That's something, huh? Love to Taft and your folk.

Fondly,

Irma

P.S. So nice of you to call Mother. She enjoyed your thoughtfulness.

---

was Irma Jackson, a social worker and WAC officer. The two women he was said to be squiring were lively Chicago "fashionables."
[*] Another Delta, my mother thinks.

Are we rich?

Mother raises those plucked, deep-toned eyebrows that did such good, expressive work for women in the 1950s. Lift the penciled arch by three to four millimeters and you had bemused doubt, blatant disdain, or disapproval just playful enough to lure the speaker into more error. Mother's lips form a small, cool smile that mirrors her eyebrow arch. She places a small, emphatic space between each word—"Are　We　Rich?"—then adds, "Why do you ask?"

I ask because I have been told that day: "Your family must be rich." A schoolmate told me and I faltered, then stalled—flattered and ashamed to be. We are supposed to eschew petty snobberies at the University of Chicago Laboratory School: intellectual superiority is our task. Other fathers are doctors. Other mothers dress well and drive stylish cars. Wondering what stirred that question has left me anxious and a little queasy.

Mother says: "We are not rich. And it's impolite to ask anyone that question. Remember that. If you're asked again, you should just say 'we're comfortable.'" I take her words in and push on, because my classmate has asked a second question.

Are we upper class?

Mother's eyebrows settle now. She sits back in the den chair and pauses for effect. I am about to receive general instruction in the liturgies of race and class.

"We're considered upper-class Negroes and upper-middle-class Americans," Mother says. "But most people would like to consider us Just More Negroes."

ii

"D. and J. asked me if we know their janitor, Mr. Johnson. They think he lives near us." (They had spoken of him so affectionately that I wished I could say I knew our janitor that well and that he liked me as much as Mr. Johnson seemed to like them. They had rights of intimacy with their janitor that I lacked.)

I have to stop here, though. My policy in these pages is to use initials when I recall the mishaps or misdeeds of my peers. Their words and acts belong to me; their names belong to them. I know initials look silly in dialogue that aims for realism. But I didn't want to use their names. They were my dear friends—one from sixth grade on, the other from our twenties on—and we grew into talking honestly about these matters. They were twins and now they're dead, killed by cancer. I didn't want them to be so starkly flawed here. But for now, they must be. And so:

"Debi and Judi asked me if we know their janitor, Mr. Johnson. They think he lives near us."

"It's a big neighborhood," Mother says. "Why would we know their janitor? White people think Negroes all know each other, and they always want you to know their janitor. Do they want to know our laundryman?"

That would be Wally, a smiling, big-shouldered white man who delivers crisply wrapped shirts and cheerful greetings to our back door every week.

"Good morning, Mrs. Jefferson," he says. "Good morning, Doctor. Hello, girls."

"Hello, Wally," we chime back from the breakfast table. Then, one weekend afternoon, I was in the kitchen with Mother doing something minor and domestic, like helping unpack groceries, when she said slowly, not looking at me: "I saw Wally at Sears today. I was looking at vacuum cleaners. And I looked up and saw him—" (Here she paused for the distancing Rodgers and Hammerstein irony, *"across a crowded room."*) "He was turning his head away, hoping he wouldn't have to speak. Wally the laundryman was trying to cut me." If this had been drama, she would have paused and done something with a telling prop— one of the better brands of an everyday food, or a nice-looking piece of flatware. Then she said, "And I don't even shop at Sears except for appliances."

Humor is laughing at what you haven't got when you ought to have it—the right, in this case, to snub or choose to speak kindly to your laundryman in a store where he must shop for clothes and you shop only for appliances.

Still, Wally went on delivering laundry with cheerful deference, and we responded with cooler—but not intrusively cool— civility.

Was there no Negro laundry to do Daddy's shirts as well or better? Our milkman was a Negro. So were our janitor, our plumber, our carpenter, our upholsterer, our caterer, and our dressmaker. Though I don't remember all their names, I know their affect was restful. Comfortable. If a Negro employee did his work in a sloppy or sullen way (and it did happen), Mother and Daddy had two responses. One was your standard folk wisecrack, something like "Well, some of us *are* lazy, quiet as it's kept." *Humor is laughing at what you haven't got when you ought to have it:* in this case, a spotless race reputation.

The second response was disquieting. "Some Negroes prefer to work for white people. They don't resent their status in the same way."

All right then, let's say you are a Negro cleaning woman, on your knees at this moment, scrubbing the bathtub with its extremely visible ring of body dirt, because whoever bathed last night thought, *How nice. I don't have to clean the tub because Cleo / Melba / Mrs. Jenkins comes tomorrow!* Tub done, you check behind the toilet (a washcloth has definitely fallen back there); the towels are scrunched, not hung on the racks, and you've just come from the children's bedroom, where sheets have to be untangled and almost throttled into shape before they can be sorted for the wash.

Would you rather look at the people you do this for and think: *I will never be in their place if the future is like the past.* Or would you rather look at your employers and think: *Well, if I'd been able to get an education like Dr. and Mrs. Jefferson, if I hadn't had to start doing housework at fifteen to help my family out when we moved up here from Mississippi, then maybe I could be where they are.*

Whose privilege would you find easier to bear?

Who are "you"? How does your sociological vita—race or ethnicity, class, gender, family history—affect your answer?

Whoever you are, reader, please understand that neither my parents, my sister, nor I ever left a dirty bathtub for Mrs. Blake to clean. (My sister and I called her Mrs. Blake. Mother called her Blake.) She was broad, not fat. She had very short, very straightened hair that she patted flat and put behind her ears. When it got humid in the basement, where the washer and dryer were, or in the room where she ironed clothes, short pieces of hair would defy hot comb and oil to stick up and out. We never made direct fun of her hair—we would have been punished. But we regularly mocked Negro hair that blatantly defied rehabilitation. Mrs. B.'s voice was Southern South Side: leisurely and nasal. Now that I've given my adult attention to the classic blues singers, I can say she had the weighted country diction of Ma Rainey and the short nasal tones of Sippie Wallace. Vowels rubbed down, end-word consonants dropped or muffled.

Mother made it clear that we were never to leave our beds unmade when Mrs. Blake was coming. She was not there to pick up after us. When we were old enough, we stripped our own beds each week and folded the linen before putting it in the hamper for her to remove and wash.

Mother's paternal grandmother, great-aunt, and aunt had been in service, so she was sensitive to inappropriate childish presumption.

Mrs. Blake ate her lunch (a hot lunch that Mother had made from dinner leftovers) in the kitchen. When her day was done, Mr. Blake and their daughters drove to our house. He sent his daughters to the front door to pick her up. They had the same initials we did. Mildred and Diane. Margo and Denise. Mother brought us to the front door to exchange hellos with them. Sometimes Mrs. Blake left carrying one or two bags of neatly folded clothes. Did Mildred and Diane enjoy unfolding, surveying, and fitting themselves into our used ensembles and separates?

"Do we have Indian blood?" I ask.

"Why are you asking?" Mother answers.

I want to know, after two weeks as a Potawatomi tribe member at the Palos Park summer camp in the Illinois Forest Preserves, being led down foot and bridle paths, sharing space with deer, birds, amphibians, and small mammals.

According to an official history of Palos Park village, Indians "roamed the hills" there in the eighteenth century, along with French explorers, traders, and soldiers, but the first white man to "settle" Palos was James Paddock, in 1834. Now, some 120 years later, Denise and Margo Jefferson have become two of the first Negro girls to attend the Palos Park camp alongside the descendants of white settlers.

And one of those descendants had asked if I had Indian blood. When I said I didn't know whether I did or not, she scanned my face and said, "You must. Ask your mother when she comes to pick you up."

On the last day of camp the little descendant stood beside me as Mother emerged from her car. Cotton piqué rose-and-white-striped dress. Light brown skin. A Claudette Colbert cap of dark hair. Beneath her black sunglasses a hooked nose asserted itself. The little descendant turned to me, nodded, and whispered, "I told you, you have Indian blood. Ask your mother on the way home."

Why should this be information I'm denied? It would be exciting to be something other than just Negro. I wait till we get home, till Denise and I have made our way through talk of cabinmates and counselors, hikes and canoe trips, through the success, achieved once more, by our normality. Then I ask my question and Mother sighs.

"Ye-sss"—drawn out to telegraph reluctance—"we do have *some* Indian blood. But I get so *tired* of Negroes always talking about their Indian blood. And *so* tired of white people always asking about it." Here's an unexpected similarity between Negroes and whites: the slightly pathetic need to believe we have Indian blood, or at least, through camp rituals, cultural kinship rights.

The next summer a full-blooded Indian comes to the camp. Denise and I take her up, enjoying her sweet manner and her dark, shining waist-length braids. Mysteriously, on the last day of camp, no one arrives to take her home. We volunteer our mother.

L. gets into the backseat with us and tells Mother where she lives. The three of us grow quiet as Mother drives, drives, and drives. Finally we arrive at a shabby group of apartment buildings. No trees, no trimmed shrubbery. We don't hug, but we say goodbye till next summer. L. gets out of the car, turns and walks toward one of the big ugly housing project buildings. She has on a rust-colored shirt and the same jeans she's worn every day at camp. Mother starts the car and speeds away. None of us says anything about L.

The next summer, neither she nor any other recognizable Indian appears at Palos Park. Another Negro does, though. R. arrives a few days after the rest of us. He's in my age group, he's a little bit chubby, and he wears glasses, not as thick as mine. He's definitely browner than I am, by several shades. He's dark brown. I notice how carefully his blue jean cuffs are rolled—folded up and ironed—and how just-from-the-package his navy and white shirt looks with its crisp, three-button collar. I know he has bad hair because it's been shaved so close to his scalp.

At the end of the week my counselor takes me aside. Can I help R. fit in better? she wants to know. Can I talk to him? Everyone is still calling him "the new kid." I'm mortified. I hate it when I'm supposed to be having fun and Race singles me out for special chores and duties. I will, I tell her, making myself sound agreeable. And I do. I can see the two of us even now, me and him, making trite, labored conversation. Neither of us smiling.

He leaves my mind after that. We had no more encounters. But here's what I want to know. Why wasn't Phillip asked to talk to R.? Because Phillip was a Negro too, and he was there for those two weeks. (Denise had graduated to the four-week Camp Martin Johnson, an interracial camp where she and a cluster of family friends established their own in-group.) Phillip was a boy, so he should have been asked to talk to Ronnie. Phillip was my friend; our parents were dear friends. Phillip had Negro hair, but it was curly, frizzy hair no one would mind patting. Phillip had pale olive skin and crisp, neatly tailored features.

"Phillip should have been asked to talk to Ronnie!" I exclaim years—decades—later, telling the story to a white friend.

"The counselors didn't read Phillip as Negro," Elizabeth says. She's seen a picture of us standing with our mothers in Washington Park. "Phillip settled into the landscape of whiteness."

Yes. We map it out. Maybe the counselors never even debated the matter. But if they did, they must have reasoned that R. would be more comfortable talking to someone who looked more like him.

I feel a surge of grief when I think of him now. And inside that grief is guilt because I looked down on him. And inside that grief is shame. Because "looked down on him" is accurate, but not sufficient.

I dreaded him.

In Negroland we thought of ourselves as the Third Race, poised between the masses of Negroes and all classes of Caucasians. Like the Third Eye, the Third Race possessed a wisdom, intuition, and enlightened knowledge the other two races lacked. Its members had education, ambition, sophistication, and standardized verbal dexterity.

—If, as was said, too many of us ached, longed, strove to be be be be White White White White WHITE . . .

—If (as was said) many us boasted overmuch of the blood *des blancs* that for centuries had found blatant or surreptitious ways to flow, course, and trickle tepidly through our veins and arteries (cephalic, aortal, renal, femoral, jugular, subclavian, and superior mesenteric) . . .

—If we placed too high a value on the looks, manners, and morals called the birthright of the Anglo-Saxon . . .

White people wanted to be white just as much as we did. They worked just as hard at it. They failed just as often. They failed more often. But they could pass, so no one objected.

Denise and Margo wear matching woolen coats with Persian lamb collars. They tuck their hands into Persian lamb muffs. They are in a state of self-enchantment. They rarely wear matching clothes, but these ones make a statement. Denise and Margo are a matching set and a set piece. Their clothes are the rewards of immaculate girlhood: dresses of taffeta and velvet with lace collars, petticoats, ankle straps, pocketbooks and initialed handkerchiefs, seasonal gloves of cotton and kid, matching coats and muffs. Straw hats and headbands with flowers. Not a single flower, corsage style, but an oval row, like a bower.

The bower of girlhood. We don't talk or laugh loudly in public. We don't slouch. Our speech is crisp and unaccented. When our aunt Ruby, a primary-school teacher, visits from California, she has me put a penny in a bank each time I say "gee." I enjoy it. I enjoy being irreproachable.

Beauty standards for girls are stringent in 1950s Negroland. Negro girls must be vigilant about their perceived deficiencies. Be ruthless. Catalogue and compensate.

- Flat feet instead of high arches.
- Obtrusive behinds that refuse to slip quietly into sheath dresses, subside, and stay put.
- "Ashy skin." White sediment on the surface of brown skin that has gone unoiled for too long. Knees and elbows must be attended to. "Elbow grease" is not a metaphor.

SKIN COLOR

Ivory, cream, beige, wheat, tan, moccasin, fawn, café au lait, and the paler shades of honey, amber, and bronze are best. Sienna, chocolate, saddle brown, umber (burnt or raw), and mahogany work best with decent-to-good hair and even-to-keen features. In these cases, the woman's wardrobe must feature subdued tones. Bright colors suggest that she is flaunting herself. Generally, for women, the dark skin shades like walnut, chocolate brown, black, and black with blue undertones are off-limits. Dark skin often suggests aggressive, indiscriminate sexual readiness. At the very least it calls instant attention to your race and can incite demeaning associations.

GRADES OF HAIR

1. *Dead* straight hair can be grown into thick, lustrous braids that stretch to the middle of the back, even to the waist.

2. Glossy hair with waves and curls: this evokes allusions to Moorish Spain and Mexico.

3. Tighter waves with a less shiny texture: this hair can be brushed almost straight but must be maintained with light hair cream. Humidity can make it rough in the back (the kitchen) and frizzy around the face. Apply quick light strokes with a hot comb.

4. Nappy hair, stage 1. Requires heavy hair cream daily and regular hot comb use. Usually does not grow past the shoulders.

5. Nappy hair, stage 2. Requires heavier and heavier applications of hair cream and constant hot comb use. Usually does not grow beyond the middle of the neck.

NOSES

The ones nobody wants are broad and flat with wide nostrils. Wide nostrils are never good, but a narrow tapering nose that ends in *flared* nostrils is acceptable, even alluring. An aquiline or hooked nose suggests American Indian ancestry. It can also be called Roman. Small, pert, upturned noses are invariably welcome.

THE JEFFERSON GIRLS

Do not have flat behinds, but theirs are cleanly shaped and not unduly full.

Neither Jefferson girl has one of the top three grades of hair.

Their mother works the hot comb and the curling iron through it. She oils it daily; besieged by rain or intense humidity, Negro hair reverts to bushy, nappy, or kinky textures. "Bushy" is the word used most; "nappy" and "kinky" are harsher, coarser words. Denise's hair is worse than Margo's by a few grades. On the other hand, when Margo was very young, she was silly enough to believe her hair would turn blonde when her mother washed it. Fortunately, she aired this belief, and it died a clean, brisk death. Hair oil can stain ribbons and headband flowers and the inside rims of pale embellished straw hats worn to church and dress events if your hands aren't clean when you put them on and take them off.

Mrs. Jefferson has a prominent Roman nose. Denise has a small, trim nose; more decorous than pert. Though Margo's nostrils flare, they do not flare in a way an unsympathetic observer could fixate on.

Both girls have full but not extravagantly full mouths. They'd prefer smaller, narrower ones, but the basic shape is clean.

No one could justly call them big-lipped.

THE JEFFERSON GIRLS AND BALLET

The elder, Denise, has a more than respectable arch, even by the demanding standards of her Scottish ballet teacher, Edna McRae. Their father's high curved arch is a thing of beauty, which his daughters study with acquisitive rapture when he stretches out on the bed after a long day at the office. Margo and her mother have flat feet.

We see every dance company that comes to Chicago: the Royal Ballet, the New York City Ballet, the Royal Danish Ballet, the Ballet Russe de Monte Carlo, American Ballet Theatre. We pore over ballet books: *A Candle for St. Jude, The Classic Ballet: Basic Technique and Terminology,* tales of *les petits rats,* the young Paris Opera Ballet students, profiles and exquisite pictures of major dancers. Alicia Markova, Margot Fonteyn, Alexandra Danilova, Maria Tallchief, Alicia Alonzo . . .

In the catalogue of physical features rendering Negroes unfit or at least unsuited for ballet, muscled, un-slender bodies figure as prominently as flat feet. There are exceptions, and we repeat their names eagerly, doggedly, dutifully.

Janet Collins, Metropolitan Opera Ballet

Raven Wilkinson, Ballet Russe de Monte Carlo

The skin of Raven Wilkinson radiated sufficient pallor to justify her inclusion in a band of twenty-four sylphs haunting the glades of a Europe basking in ethereal melancholy, their bodies mere extensions of luminous white tulle and satin. Janet Collins had an epidermal undertone that ruined visual and narrative consistency onstage. She had been accepted by the Ballet Russe de Monte Carlo on condition that she paint her face and limbs white. She refused, packed her leotards and tights, and left the building. Instead she set her feet on the roads that led to race- and myth-driven musicals (*Run, Little Chillun', The Swing Mikado, Out of This World*) and to modern dance, where small groups of Negroes and Asians performed on the stages of Ys and civic auditoriums, often beside those ethnic Caucasians (Jews and Catholics) less likely to have found their way to ballet.

She was thirty-four years old in 1951, when the Metropolitan Opera Ballet selected her to embody heroines in operatic interludes set among French gypsies, Ethiopian royals, and biblical Semites. It was groundbreaking, though everyone knew the Metropolitan Opera Ballet was not a first-rate company. It was an auxiliary, a subsidiary. (*They always wait till you're past your prime*, our parents and our Negro journalists complain. *The Metropolitan Opera didn't invite Marian Anderson to make her debut there till 1954. She was the gypsy fortune-teller in* A Masked Ball *and she was fifty-eight years old.*)

Denise was seven in 1951 when she told our mother she wanted to take ballet lessons. Serious ones. Till then, she spent her time at the Beatrice Betts Ballet School playing with friends and fluffing up her tutu. Mother consulted artistic Negro friends who knew about the best white teachers and who among them was most likely to take a non-white student.

Your daughter has real talent, says Miss Edna McRae, whose studio was downtown in the Fine Arts Building. *Still, considering onstage convention and offstage prejudice, she will probably have to dance with an all-Negro modern company like Katherine Dunham's.* We aren't ashamed of Katherine Dunham, we're proud; she is a worthy dance pioneer with a university education, and not a minor university either: the University of Chicago, our mother's school. Her Caribbean and African dances are based on her PhD research into the culture and folklore of those regions. "Folklore" is the word generally used. It suggests tradition, but it's a few tiers below "civilization." No matter how much formal training they have, no matter how hard they study and practice, these dancers/performers are enacting rituals many in their audience believe are driven more by biology than by art. Why, then, with some of the best ballet training Chicago possessed, would Denise choose to do what most Americans believed it was her body's natural inclination to do? Especially since her teacher warned that it was probably her only option?

Denise has a talent and an arch. Her feet curve becomingly in pointe shoes.

THE JEFFERSON GIRLS AND BEAUTY

Denise's skin is burnt sienna. Margo and her mother are café au lait, and the blue veins in their hands can be seen by anyone. Which, on a timeline stretching back to post-Reconstruction, would secure their membership in the best Negro churches and clubs; ensure their presence at events like the 1930s dinner dance given by a Washington, D.C., men's club that called itself the What Good Are We's. "Don't bring any brown-skinned girls," his host told their burnt sienna bachelor father, who was doing his internship in Baltimore. And he did not. No ladies browner than Margo and her mother were present that night, and their numbers were scant. Pale beige, cream, and ivory, even alabaster, were on abundant, radiant display.

When they watch the Miss America pageant, her daughters do not find Mrs. Jefferson lacking in any way.

"Mama, you could be a Miss America!" they cry one morning when she picks them up from a rapturous night spent watching the contest at their grandmother's. Their mother's laugh deflects them, as does their grandmother's smile. (*These children know so little about the world. We won't lecture and disillusion them, but we won't encourage this line of thinking; we'll change the subject.*) The two of them know exactly who is beautiful, who is pretty, and who is *attractive* by the national beauty standard. "Attractive" is a word for women who've made the most of their assets, but whose assets aren't enough to make them pretty or beautiful. They know what clothes play up their strengths, what makeup mutes their flaws. Mother considers herself attractive. She and Grandma believe that most Negro women are considered, at best, attractive.

A few years later, still faithfully watching the pageant, Denise and Margo feel acute disappointment when Miss Hawaii, who clearly has native ancestry, does not place among the finalists. She's named Miss Congeniality instead. And Mother decides it's high time we know the story of her sorority sister Geraldine.

Geraldine was a beauty by all objective standards. We'd seen her at Mother's club meetings, her keen symmetrical features, her gleaming hair with waves like Jane Russell's, her Mexican-brown complexion. Geraldine had won the Cap and Gown beauty contest when she was a student at the University of Chicago. She was a serious young woman, so she hadn't campaigned for it; she'd been nominated by a male friend who hadn't asked her permission. Still, she won the most votes.

And then university officials realized that she was one of their Negro students and had her disqualified.

She'd never wanted it, she always said.

And she never forgave them for taking it from her.

Equal opportunity should mean that an audience of Americans would be ready, willing, and eager when you, an unimpeachably outstanding Negro woman, stepped forth to stir, win, command their admiration.

Truly heroic women achieved fame by putting the needs of others first, however. This demanded unceasing fortitude and the renunciation of all things lighthearted. This demanded the renunciation of vanity.

Two large elderly women in large antique chairs take up the October 1955 cover of *Ebony* magazine. Their suits have straight, undeviating, and ankle-shielding skirts. Small, inadequate hats sit on their heads. They have no interest in the pink corsages pinned to their shoulders. One is a Negro, and she will never be on the cover of *Life* magazine; the other is a Caucasian who has been there twice: She is making a gracious and noteworthy guest appearance at *Ebony*. Mary McLeod Bethune is the Negro, broad and stout. Lanky, big-boned Eleanor Roosevelt is the Caucasian. When attractive women in suits cross their legs at the knee, we see a shapely column of thigh draped in fabric, then a second, bared column of flesh. These two women seem to have no legs. They have wide laps. Their hands rest there, as do the troubles of the world.

Surely they look like this because they have been working day and night, years, struggling to defeat the forces of prejudice and ignorance. Working to prove that people like us deserve our rights. They have renounced the feminine privileges we are learning at our mothers' shapely knees. Still, our mothers want us to honor Mrs. Bethune. Without such women, they say, we would not have the opportunity to be nice Negro girls whose mothers are ladies.

Another Negro History Week Lesson

Mary Jane McLeod was born in a small log cabin to hard-working farmers who had been slaves. With the help of their seventeen children, the McLeods of South Carolina farmed their five acres diligently. Some days Mrs. McLeod earned extra money by cooking for the family of her former master. She would often bring little Mary along on these visits, and it happened that one day the nine-year-old, bored perhaps, or lonely, wandered out to the playhouse, where the white children were studying. Her eyes swept over a host of unfamiliar objects—pencils, slates, books, magazines; as her hand reached out to claim one, a voice said, "You can't read that—put it down," then added more kindly, "I will show you some pictures over here." It was too late. The black child had been mortified—into ambition.

Intensely ambitious and smart little girls from humble backgrounds need the protective coloration of cheerful spirits, and religious faith. They must work unceasingly when they win scholarships to Negro seminaries and white Bible colleges; they must make clear that no task is too lowly, no request unwelcome. A plain and cheerful face is useful too: it helps endear such a child to all female schoolteachers (Negro and white) intent on promoting the doctrines of modesty and humility; it can shield her from any male instructors who might be gripped by desires they have been encouraged to act out with colored girls.

Mary made herself a favorite at every school she attended.

She would boast, in later years, that she was of pure, undefiled African stock, descended on her mother's side from a nation of female rulers. In early years she did not boast. She practiced deference, duty, and decorum. And she made sure to excel.

She longed to go to Africa as a missionary. The Baptist Mission Service informed her that they had no place in Africa for a Negro missionary, so she returned to the American South and became a missionary to young black girls threatened by poverty, ignorance, and degradation. She built a matriarchal kingdom from the ramshackle materials of Negro life in Florida.

In the year 1904 Mary McLeod Bethune (by then a wife and mother) opened her Daytona Educational and Industrial Training Institute on a former garbage site, in a cabin scrubbed and swept clean for five little girls who would learn reading, writing, cooking, sewing, and health and hygiene; would be converted from indigence to competence and be offered propriety in place of promiscuity. Her husband was not especially supportive; three years later they parted ways.

Footnote to Negro History Lesson:

Little Carrie Butler of South Carolina was five years old when Mrs. Bethune opened her school. Had her parents been able to send her nearly 575 miles to Daytona, in 1925 sixteen-year-old Carrie might have been preparing to graduate. She might have been standing proudly in the doorway of a building called Faith Hall, ready to weave rugs, cane chairs, and raise poultry in the home with her husband, ready to teach other young girls how to turn domestic labor into the principles of domestic science, ready to become a nurse. Instead she would become an unwed mother that year, bearing the female child of the twenty-five-year-old lawyer Strom Thurmond Jr., whose parents employed her as a maid.

By 1927 Mrs. Bethune had turned her little school into a bona fide college. Then she founded the National Council of Negro Women and fought for our rights year after year, fought to prove to a doubting country that we were hardworking and high-minded, bent on improving ourselves, our communities, and our families. Lifting us as we climbed out of the chasm of history.

When Franklin Roosevelt collected a small group of prominent, highly accomplished Negroes for his "Black Cabinet," she was the only woman.

Children being the agreed-on provenance of all accomplished women, she was sent to the National Youth Administration. Negroes being judged qualified advisers on few affairs other than their own, she directed the Division of Negro Youth. Through her National Council of Negro Women, Bethune managed to diversify: members turned their energies to politics, jobs, housing, and civil rights. Just as Eleanor Roosevelt was doing from her secure domain as first lady.

They are old now, Mrs. Bethune and Mrs. Roosevelt. They always looked this way, though, even when they were young and photographed wearing velvet and crepe de chine, strands of pearls and garnets circling their necks and falling down their sloping bosoms. The upswept hair, the shapely little hats are like a nervous decorator's afterthoughts in a gloomy house. Nothing could soften Mrs. Bethune's broad nose and dark skin; temper the pale wrinkles and faltering chin of Mrs. Roosevelt.

Yet we owe women like this our lives.

And their worthiness numbs even as it stirs us.

Even in 1955, at the age of eight, I am not interested in

Bethune-Cookman College. Even that early, I know my sister and I would never be sent there. Everyone knows President Roosevelt was much better looking than his wife. This is not a position my friends and I want to be in when we marry. We can't achieve what Mrs. Roosevelt did, so we'll just pay for being plain.

Denise is in our parents' bedroom, at Mother's vanity dresser. She tries on earrings and necklaces; she hazards a provocative smile; she puts her right elbow on the glass-covered dresser top and places her chin on her hand. (Her ballet class hand, soft but alert and slightly rounded.) Before dinner she will ask: "Who do I look more like, Lena Horne or Dorothy Dandridge?"

I am listening to records. *Guys and Dolls, The King and I, Oklahoma!* . . . I perform rake bravado, soubrette whimsy, judicious womanliness. The beautiful young lieutenant from Main Line Philadelphia has found himself in love with a beautiful brown-skinned girl in the South Pacific. She is Polynesian and speaks no English. (We know, though the rest of America may not, that Juanita Hall, who plays her mother, is really a Negro.)

The lieutenant has learned a lesson I already know, a lesson he sings about with the fearless, legato insistence of the wholly sheltered. "You've got to be taught to be afraid / Of people whose eyes are oddly made." Singing along, I make the "oddly" more staccato and curl my lip. His "And people whose skin is a different shade" is earnest, impassioned. I keep the passion but mute the earnestness with a raised eyebrow.

It's weekend television time.

Sammy Davis Jr. is going to be on *The Milton Berle Show*.

Dorothy Dandridge is going to be on *The Jerry Lewis Colgate Comedy Hour*.

Lena Horne is going to be on *The Frank Sinatra Timex Show*.

These are seminal moments in the viewing mores of the nation.

After dinner, the four of us gather in the TV room. Our parents are on the couch; Denise and I push the hassocks as near to the TV as we can, or stretch out on the floor till we're told to sit up.

"Ladies and gentlemen, please welcome . . ."

Sammy Davis Jr. does a swing-run onto the stage. He wears a taut, close-fitting suit and rectangular black-framed glasses.

My parents saw him live in New York.

My father: "He can do it all!"

My mother: "He certainly can." (Pause.) "He still has too much oil in his hair."

They've talked about how men in show business tend to use too much oil or oil that's too thick. These men don't always use stocking caps either, which settle the hair into thin ridge-waves that don't have to pretend to be straight.

Sammy can dance (beautifully) and sing (very well). He enunciates crisply, with no trace of a stock Negro accent. He imitates the racially neutral vocal stylings of Nat King Cole and Billy Daniels *and* the racially white vocal stylings of Cary Grant, James Stewart, and James Cagney. This is cheeky and very satisfying. Daddy sits back on the couch. We hear him chuckle. Mother leans forward eagerly and tips her cigarette into the aquamarine glass ashtray.

Sammy isn't on his own, though—not yet. He is followed onstage by two quiet, portly, balding men. He is still tethered to his father, Sammy Davis Sr., and to the kind employer of his childhood he still calls "Uncle Will." He is still part of the Will Mastin Trio.

"He's carrying them along," Mother comments impatiently. The older men have the generic smiles of vaudeville second-stringers who learned years ago how to frame the star, keep time, recede, do their specialty step, recede, and exit—from stage and memory. They speak with mild and genial Negro accents. They're from an age before television, before Broadway theaters like Ed Sullivan's, where cheerful white people sat, eager to be entertained; before TV rec rooms, before dens where Negro families sat waiting to be entertained and hoping not to be denigrated. Will Mastin and Sammy Davis Sr. are folk art before folk art becomes museum-worthy.

"It's time for them to go," my father says in a gentle, definite way.

Lena Horne's nostrils flare; they do not spread. The bridge of her nose is thin and exact. The nose of Dorothy Dandridge is a little bit fuller, but it's not *full*. And she has a dimple right above her lips. Cupid's-bow lips. Maidenly lips. Lena's smile is wide, but her lips are not. She has high, wide Indian cheekbones, so she needs a wide smile. Her top lip is so narrow that she probably has trouble applying lipstick properly. Like my grandmother.

Lena and Dorothy can wear their hair any way they want. Upswept with bangs and tendrils, like Jennifer Jones; shoulder-length with wave clusters, like Elizabeth Taylor; trimmed to a cap of wayward curls, like Ava Gardner, who's from the South and may have black blood. They look glamorous; they look comfortable in evening gowns and fur stoles. Like Mother and her friends. But most people don't know we Negroes dress like that.

———

Dorothy Dandridge sings in a studio-set apartment. When a woman sings on a television show she's supposed to be singing in her cute living room or her frilly boudoir. There's a window frame with curtains behind her. She's waiting for her gentleman friend. She can peer into a mirror and pout. She can perch on a small cushioned chair and kick her legs up. She can fling herself onto a love seat. She can pick up a real poodle when the song ends and hug it coquettishly.

Dorothy Dandridge wears a pale ruffled ball gown in her single-miss apartment. She has put her hair in a society-hostess bun with a center part. There are four strands of pearls around her neck. She looks down, as if she's misbehaved, then lifts her head and smiles.

"Blow out the candle," she sings pertly,

> Blow out the candle,
> Blow out the candle so the neighbors won't see!

She cups her hands at her waist, clasps them at her throat—opera singers always do this on TV—throws her head back just a bit, and smiles again. She extends an arm, then flings it up and flicks her wrist. It's almost Spanish! Her shoulders move slightly, no more than a few measures, and off the beat. Then she sways her hips, pretending not to notice that they're swaying. ("Just enough," says my mother.) She mimes snuffing out a candle like French maids do in operas.

> Won't you blow out the candle,
> So there will be no scandal?

And no one will know
You've been ki-i-i-ssing me!

"Why couldn't they give her a real song? Ellington or a show tune," my father wants to know. He doesn't want to know; he knows, and we know too. "She did the best she could do with that ditty."

But Lena Horne has made her way into the show-tune penthouse. Lena Horne sings Cole Porter. She's wearing a black sheath with full-length, see-through sleeves. The white curtains behind her curl and drape.

"While tearing off a game of golf . . ." Hah!

My father doesn't care about golf, but plenty of his friends do.

The collar of her sheath is made of tulle netting, and it matches the cuffs. Tulle ruffles cuff her wrists. Lena Horne doesn't move her body at all. She stands in profile the whole time. Her behind is perfectly round, not big. One arm is poised at her waist. The other moves stealthily toward the fancy chair that goes with a vanity dresser that isn't on the set.

She places her wrist on the chair back with extreme care. ("Hauteur" is my mother's word.) She has ballet hands, but they're a little pointed. They're show business ballet hands. She lets two fingers touch the curve of the chair and move back and forth.

"Ah just adore his asking for more . . ." This time the "I" is "Ah," while "adore" comes out "adoharr" and "more" (her eyes widen and stare out on "more") rolls itself into "mohrr."

The syllables stay crisp, though. They're not guttural. They're a design carved onto the surface of each word. She stretches her mouth open, widens it and shows her teeth. Even and gleaming in perfect formation. She smiles but curls her lips as she sings "But my heart belongs to Daddy." She turns her face away and lifts her chin. For the last line—" 'cause my daddy, he treats it so well"—we see only her profile.

My parents talk about what she does with her face. Lena mugs, they agree, but she can get away with it. She's a beauty.

And she used to be bland. Then she married Lennie Hayton. He was a bandleader and arranger, a big wheel at MGM. He gave her sophisticated arrangements and taught her how to put a song over with personality, with pizzazz. To rule it, not defer to it.

Lennie Hayton is white, but when you see pictures of them in *Ebony,* he's the one who looks grateful. He's always smiling. He's standing behind her most of the time, with his white hair and little beard. Lena knew what she was doing.

She never has the lapses in taste Dorothy Dandridge has. One Sunday night on *Ed Sullivan* the curtains part to show Dorothy in a strapless gown that pushes her breasts up and toward each other and out toward the waiting audience. In a whispery voice, sometimes closing her eyes and sliding her head back toward undulating shoulders, she chants, "He's a smooth operator, a cool sweet potato and a gone alligator."

> I'm here to tell you
> One natural fact
> (*CHA* cha cha *CHA CHA CHA CHA!*)
> I like it like that!
> You drive me wild
> You make me shout
> Have mercy Mister Percy
> Now cut that out!

"Mercy Mister Percy?" my mother repeats when Ed Sullivan has extended his arm, thanked Miss Dandridge, and gone to a commercial break. "Why doesn't she just say 'Master' and sing it standing on an auction block?"

Everybody knows Dorothy Dandridge wants to marry a white man. *She's never managed to turn a white lover into a loving husband, and she'll never stop trying.* Everyone knows Otto Preminger won't marry her, though she hoped he would after he directed *Carmen Jones* and she became the first Negro woman to get an Academy Award nomination for best actress. Carmen was a wanton, which we resent seeing Negro women play since most people think that's what Negro women are, but at least Carmen started out as a gypsy in a French opera.

Two years later Dorothy Dandridge was supposed to play Tuptim in *The King and I*—Tuptim the refined Burmese maiden pledged to the king of Siam by her ambitious father, yet loving the gently handsome Lun Tha, to whom she was first betrothed.

But Dorothy Dandridge turned the role down: Tuptim was little more than a slave, she declared. And how the Negro establishment lauded her decision. So Dorothy Dandridge denied hundreds of Negro girls the chance to sit rapturously in a movie theater watching a *Negro woman* pad delicately across palace floors in Oriental silk (turquoise, fuchsia, emerald green, and gold), voice sweetly chanting, eyes faintly slanted, and hair straight and dark as a raven's wing. Exquisite, chastely arousing; worthy of worship, anguish, sacrifice. Played instead by the Puerto Rican Rita Moreno.

What misbegotten scruples! The enthrallment of a beautiful Asian woman is not squalid; it is refined through ancient rituals of the Orient that white people must acknowledge despite their racial and cultural misgivings. We Negroes long for such an aura. When my school stages a musical revue that year that includes "The March of the Siamese Children," I get to be one, in red sateen, with a topknot, rouged cheeks and lipstick, eyes drawn to a wide slant with a teacher's blunt makeup pencil. A year later, I watch the Japanese Miiko Taka enchant Marlon Brando in *Sayonara*. He wants to marry her, and in the end he does. It's profoundly exciting.

Two years after *The King and I,* Dorothy Dandridge will be playing a Negro slave in *Tamango* and a drug-addled wanton in *Porgy and Bess,* torn between a brute, a pimp, and a crippled beggar. She will marry a white man no one has heard of—referred to in the Negro and white press as a restaurateur or nightclub proprietor. My parents mock husbands of stars with undistinguished résumés; usually they're described as their wives' managers. Jack Dennison runs some kind of restaurant in Las Vegas, and will soon be opening one in Los Angeles. What kind of *restaurateuring* did he do before he met Dorothy Dandridge with her money and Hollywood connections? He'd never be able to get a white wife of her stature, would he?

Every month I study the *Ebony* magazines that appear in our den. Chronicles of achievement and admiration, sought, won, thwarted, denied. Wonder Books of sociology.

The most successful Negro celebrities are written up in *Life* and *Look* too. But *Life* and *Look* don't have these constant debates with themselves and their readers (whom they don't need to call "their people"). *Life* and *Look* affirm and defend norms they are sure of; in *Ebony* we strive to establish norms and be lauded for those we maintain. Normality. We proclaim it, and fight for it on racial and nonracial grounds. And yet, we proclaim our designated abnormalities at every turn.

Racial Believe-It-or-Not: " 'White' Mother to Negro Twins"; "Fla. Sheriff Calls White Family Black"; "The Secret Life of an Ex-Negro"; "British Foster Mother: London Housewife Has Cared for More Negro Children than Any Other English Woman"; "The Girl Without a Race."

What manner of man and woman are we? Wherever we go we disrupt order.

Race Social Psychology: "Problems of Blond Negroes"; "What Africans Think of Us"; "Where Mixed Couples Live"; "Is the Negro Happy?"

Nothing about us is taken for granted by anyone anywhere in the world.

Uplift and Advancement: "The North's Biggest Negro Business"; "Virginia's First Negro Medical Grad"; "Tennis Queen from Harlem"; "Negro Architect Builds Sinatra Home"; "College Calendar Girl: Negro Coed Wins Cover Girl Spot at Southern Illinois U."

"Negro" is the magic word, the spell. The small grow large, the mundane turns exceptional, and the individual becomes cosmic.

Portents and Losses: "Are There Too Many Negroes in Baseball?"; "Are Negro Businessmen Through?"; " 'Why I Quit My TV Show,' by Nat King Cole, as told to Lerone Bennett, Jr." ("For 18 months I was the Jackie Robinson of television . . . The men who dictate what Americans see and hear didn't want to play ball"); "Negro Progress in 1959: Still Marked by Massive Resistance."

Society can turn any success of ours into a setback; permit us to advance, then insist that we fail or, on pain of death, retreat.

Was I correct in remembering that Louis Armstrong wrote a story called "Why I Like Dark Women"? Yes, here it is, the cover story of *Ebony*'s August 1954 issue, in capital letters. Louis's wife, Lucille, smiles up at him, chipper and chubby and dark of hue, sure of her dimples, sure of herself. Nearly his walnut brown, but with a touch more red. (Twenty years before, Lucille had crossed the color line at New York's celebrated and segregated Cotton Club to become the first *brown*-skinned

dancer in its exclusively "Tall, Tan and Terrific" chorus line.)
Three months before her husband tells readers why he likes dark
women, the Supreme Court bans segregation in public schools.

This particular article stayed with me because I found the
title embarrassing then; it wasn't the proclaimed taste of the
world I knew, and I had more than an inkling of the lewd sneer
behind the phrase "dark meat."

Now when I read the article it's clear Louis and Lucille are
telling Negroes we mustn't let the darker hues of our life and
history be erased by the demands of integration. Just at the time
nine Supreme Court justices were explaining to white Americans Why We Must Tolerate Dark Children.

December 1954: Again, my recollection is correct. There is a
lead story explaining "Why Negroes Don't Like Eartha Kitt."
I adore Eartha Kitt. I know every word of "Monotonous," her
fancifully, outrageously jaded hit song from Broadway's *New
Faces of 1952*. The article says Miss Kitt doesn't just do business
in the suave, celebrated world of white supper clubs and Broadway openings, she also chooses to socialize there. The Negro
reporter is sympathetic: he says she prefers her own kind of integration to the soigné segregation of upper-crust parties in Harlem or Bronzeville. Negroes must learn to respect a woman who
"insisted on winning fame as a raceless star rather than a Negro
entertainer." Negroes must learn to accept a woman whose difficult childhood—she was poor and illegitimate, passed from
relative to relative in the South, looked down on by whites, and
mocked by her own people because she had light brown skin
and mixed blood—had made her difficult. Touchy. Those of
us going forward in the white world need to understand Eartha
Kitt's complexes.

In the *Ebony* photograph, Eartha Kitt's brown torso is sheathed in white beads and turned toward the camera. One hand, with its multi-stone ring and triangle-tip nails, nearly caresses her chin; the other holds a beaded fan, white but no whiter than the tips of her teeth that show through parted red lips. When *New Faces* arrives in Chicago, my parents' friends patronize the show. Led by Kay Davis Wimp, who'd sung with Duke Ellington, they meet its clever producer, Leonard Sillman. And my parents take the unusual step of throwing a party for the cast.

Miss Kitt is the only significant cast member who does not attend.

Her absence stung. She embodied our daydreams about ourselves—the cheeky glamour, the impossibly suave accent, as if she'd been conceived between Mayfair and Casablanca. "Monotonous" slithered through and past social and sexual prohibitions as she languidly declared herself the world's most desirable woman, utterly bored by all that the world's most powerful men—including T. S. Eliot, King Farouk, and President Eisenhower—could offer. "Sherman Billingsley cooks for me / Monotonous," she crooned, the year after he made world headlines for refusing to seat the still-desirable Josephine Baker at his swanky Stork Club.

We'd been insulted. My parents and their friends said it showed she was insecure about her own humble origins and didn't want to risk being around Negro professionals. Their accomplishments would remind her that show business glamour did not trump family or education.

But she'd still managed to cut us.

Monotonous.

Sit on the stairs with Denise and me as our parents give one of their parties. The music on the record player might be Ellington (the suave heft of "In a Mellow Tone"). Or Erroll Garner's "Autumn Leaves." Rhapsodic, then antic and sly.

Jewelry glistens. So does the ice in cocktail glasses. Women lean in to have their cigarettes lit. Their voices run along the treble scale. And the men: the Arthur Prysock baritone with its undulating Southernness; the Northern leading-man diction of Billy Eckstine; the patter and murmur of Nat King Cole. Standard to blues English and back again, like Joe Williams.

Two of the handsomest men spot us and insist we come to the bottom of the stairs to be kissed on the cheek. Everett White, with his rich brown skin, his dimples, his white hair with its tiny crisp waves. Ed Wimp, ivory-pale with keen features and straight dark hair.

The Basie Band strides through "Corner Pocket." I settle back on the stairs, just below Denise, pressing my glasses against the banister.

Every little girl looks for something to hate about herself, and I hated my glasses.

As my father told it, he was sitting on the back porch when he heard Mother sobbing loudly. She was coming out of the garage with me in her arms. I may have added to the din, not knowing the cause but panicked by our role reversal.

I was two years old and we'd been to the eye doctor. His diagnosis was myopia, astigmatism, and strabismus, which meant I was nearsighted with blurred vision and eyes that crossed. (Maybe that's why I had recently crashed into a small table and broken several cups of a lovely tea set.) Dr. Richardson prescribed glasses with such a high correction that the lenses jutted out of the frames by a good half inch. My eyes were blurred dots behind them.

I had an operation when I was four. It helped, but I had to wear a black patch in first grade to maintain strength in my lazy eyes. I was not alone: two other girls wore patches. But Millicent had wavy hair, pert features, dimpled cheeks, and reddish-brown skin that made mine look tepid. Mimi had keen features, creamy beige skin that made mine look dark, and hair straight enough for a darling pixie cut. We all wore variations on the same theme: plastic cat's-eye with a clear bottom and bright top (red was my favorite); plastic cat's-eye in a solid color or jaunty pattern (candy stripes were popular). Some solid colors had designs—small dots or leaves—on their tips. Everything to make what was not cute cute.

In sixth grade I wore a patch again, on alternate eyes. Patches were flesh-colored by then, an improvement that felt like no improvement at all. No one else wore one.

People still mention my glasses when they catalogue their youthful memories of me. "You wore such thick glasses! I can still see you in those glasses!" I hate their benignly humorous tone. Why can't they shut up about it?

I got contact lenses the summer after my freshman year in high school. That was my jubilant entrance into Attractiveness.

I looked at myself in the mirror with hope and satisfaction. Eye-liner and mascara registered. My good figure was an advantage, not compensation. The small group of boys who'd called me "Blind"—"Hey Blind, what's happening?" they'd say in easy, jocular tones—grew more respectfully playful.

When I feel sure of myself I sometimes joke that in ancient times, when tribes faced hard survival choices, my eyes would have meant I'd be left on a hilltop to die, along with the wounded, the aged, and the mentally deficient.

I do think (and I regret this as a writer) that part of my sensory equipment has been stunted. Early on, I theorize, I stopped counting on my visual acuity, and that meant I ceased to register certain visual impressions. And despite all the care I like taking with my appearance, despite my love of fashion, despite my vanity, when I'm most at my ease with people, all kinds of people, I catch myself thinking that I'm not physically visible, that whoever I'm talking to is responding to my personality, not my person.

This began, I think, as a way—and not a bad way—for me to feel less self-conscious while marked by an eye patch and thick specs. I always measured myself against my Negro friends, and even when we had the same basic equipment (skin shade, hair grade, feature size and shape), my glasses put me at a disadvantage. With my white friends at the Lab School I managed an illusory respite. Of course I measured myself against the girls; of course I did. But if I wasn't really being seen, how could I been seen as irreversibly different?

Our parents wanted us to go to first-rate private schools. The two in Chicago that accepted Negroes in those years were Francis Parker and the University of Chicago Laboratory School. (Once conjoined, they'd since become amiable rivals.) Lab was founded by the pragmatist philosopher John Dewey in 1896, just two years after the university. Along with progressive reformers like Horace Mann and Jane Addams, he wanted education to be a creative, idealistic social enterprise, not a series of lessons absorbed by rote. "The child, not the lesson, is the center of the teacher's attention," he said; a classroom should nurture experimentation and individual talent; feature activities—field trips, nature study, open-ended discussions and activities (if you studied the tomato, you made tomato bisque)—that "reflect the life of the larger society, . . . permeated throughout with the spirit of art, history, and science." It was a coeducational mono-racial institution in a pristinely, quietly vigilant white neighborhood.

The University High School was founded in 1904. It too was coeducational and mono-racial: racial reform was launched in the early years of the Second World War. "Democracy in education was an important theme," write the authors of the school's official history, *Experiencing Education: 100 Years of Learning at the University of Chicago Laboratory Schools,* and one group of parents "used the example of racism in Europe to address racial discrimination at home."

Two teachers gave an interdisciplinary course on "minority problems," which included an interracial panel of tenth graders from Lab and the mostly Negro DuSable High School. It was an urban exchange program in a fiercely segregated city, and while it was deemed a success, there were excruciating moments. Before the Negro students arrived, recalled Lab teacher Edith Shepherd, "we suggested that we begin by giving the visitors Cokes or punch. We met with instant shock and opposition from a few students in our group." Negroes? "It was perfectly all right in their minds to have discussions with these students, but to have a social affair was quite different and we had to use quite a bit of persuasion with a few who couldn't see partaking of refreshments with them."

With a majority backing from the Parents Association, four Negro students were admitted in 1942. In 1951 Denise entered Lab's second-grade class, after a year at the all-Negro Rosenwald Nursery School and first grade at the all-Negro St. Edmund's Episcopal Day School. The next year, with no prior school experience, I entered Lab's kindergarten.

Each morning, Mother would drive us from our home in Park Manor to our school in Hyde Park.

Most of the Chicago neighborhoods I remember as pristinely Negro were pristinely white when Negroes like my parents moved in. Young men just out of the largely segregated army; young women newly married, ready to become mothers. All with their hard-earned pride and privilege: doctors, lawyers, businessmen, accountants, principals and teachers, social workers and socialites. The South Side's one integrated neighborhood—Hyde Park–Kenwood—was under strict surveillance by the University of

Chicago, which made sure that class likeness compensated for race difference. Integration meant a small number of bourgeois blacks amid bourgeois whites who'd decided their presence was acceptable. A very few Negro families lived nearly alone in a very few tenuously integrated suburbs. They drove into the city for the social events considered basic for their children's social health.

My South Side felt benign and orderly in my childhood. But there was an undercurrent of drama, excitement. In any city, the "good" and "bad" neighborhoods as your parents define them—who you play with comfortably, who you don't, the well-designed houses, the slipshod ones, the pleasant greetings, the dirty looks, feeling you're indulged, feeling you're resented—are separated by blocks, half blocks, turned corners.

Still, in certain places it felt like we were all Negroes together, holding forth in food shops, bakeries, shoe stores; hanging out on street corners, music bursting and drifting out of record stores and restaurants. Forty-Seventh and South Park: we got our hair done at Stormy's Beauty Shop. Sixty-Third and Cottage Grove: Jesse Miller, our dentist, had his office there, near the El tracks. It was "My people onstage—sound, color, action!" Negro men in loud clothes and extravagant caps making percussive sounds on street corners, *Wha-ht?* or *Wha-hh? Whoo* (high-pitched). *Ummm Ummnn Ummn* (lightly conveying *"What a shame, but let's move on"*). Emphatic but more legato *"Un-UNn-nh . . ."*

The laugh. (Hands clap, feet shuffle or lightly stomp forward and back, body bent over; go into squat and rise; bend knees a few times quickly; return to loose standing position.)

Bliss.

Once in a seizure of excitement at 63rd and Cottage Grove I asked my mother if she felt that way. Yes, she said, she'd always felt that way about 47th and South Park.

———

We were Bronzeville girls until I was three and Denise six; then we moved to Park Manor. Bronzeville was the second biggest Negro city in America, and our grandmother owned two buildings there. We were living comfortably in one of them on a day in 1949 when history records that "the attempt by two black families to move into two houses in the South Side neighborhood of Park Manor produced a mob of 2000 whites chanting 'We Want Fire, We Want Blood,' while white policemen watched in silence."* What else would White Policemen do? They were upholding twenty-five years of law and more than one hundred years of custom. They were protecting the property of their fellow officers who owned homes in Park Manor.

One evening several years later, when we have safely settled in Park Manor, a patrol car stops Daddy on his way home.

"What are you doing here?"

"I live here."

"What's in that black bag? Drugs?"

"I'm a doctor."

Which the bag's contents reveal he is. A pediatrician, luckily, not an anesthesiologist.

---

* The words that follow read "Crosses were burned and the two houses were stoned." I couldn't bear to place them on the same page with all the rest. I'm so sick of that burning cross: I hate that it's a cliché of bigotry, drama that never loses its real-life power. But how many times can you read about it? The stones are more shocking. More primal and foreign—I can't protect myself against their shock and power. But there's something else too. I want to shield my father, even though he's dead. He and his family fled Mississippi in 1918 and settled in California a few years later. They purchased a home in what he later called "a modest white working-class neighborhood." A cross was burned on their lawn the day they moved in. My grandfather sat on the porch of his new Los Angeles home all night holding the same gun he'd once pulled on a group of recalcitrant white men in Coffeeville, Mississippi. And then the plot shifted. The family sued, went to court, and won the right to keep their house.

But that was not a story told to children. It was not told because:

> The question of the child's future is a serious dilemma for Negro parents. Awaiting each colored child are cramping limitations and buttressed obstacles in addition to those that must be met by youth in general; and this dilemma approaches suffering in proportion to the parents' knowledge of and the child's ignorance of these conditions. Some parents up to the last moment strive to spare the child the bitter knowledge; the child of less sensitive parents is likely to have this knowledge driven in upon him from infancy. And no parent may definitely say which is the wiser course, for either of them may lead to spiritual disaster for the child.

The child, yes. But what about the parents, who must relive their bitter knowledge; who might have buried it till the child's need moment bears down on them to force it up and out, or back down once more? Either may lead to spiritual disaster for the parent.

We have bought an apartment house. Three of the four floors are ours. We rent the fourth to a divorcée, Mrs. Collins (Negro), who makes hats and who walks through her apartment in bright filmy robes and mules with swansdown trim. She smokes, and slurs her words with husky precision. Like Peggy Lee singing "Black Coffee."

To our left is round-faced, genial Dr. Hall (Negro), who wears a brown felt fedora in winter and a pale straw one in summer. I would say that his complexion was dark tobacco. Jesse Owens (famous Negro athlete) lives at the end of the block for a time but takes his children to another pediatrician. In the pale stone house on the other side are Mr. and Mrs. Willie Hull. They have lightly Southernized voices. Mr. Hull is a cabdriver. Mrs. Hull is a nurse with full bangs and shoulder-length dark curls. Their daughter Shirley is my age; we often play together in her backyard or mine.

Now nobody burns crosses, or twists their face into ugly grimaces and shouts. We're coming, and the neighborhood is going. *Brrring* goes the telephone up and down each block. "Hello, we're savvy white realtors and you're angry white homeowners. Let us buy your houses now and sell them to the Negroes at much higher prices than you or any other white person would pay. You'll be laughing all the way to the bank. Let them pay to ruin the neighborhood if they want it so much."

"Mother, were there ever white families on our block?" I ask twenty years later.

"Oh yes, my child, they were there. There was one right next door before the Hulls came. They had two children. About your age. And they encouraged them to have as little as possible to do with you girls."

One Summer Day in 1952...

Mrs. Jefferson put Denise and Margo in bed for their afternoon nap, then went downstairs to the breakfast room. She sat at the table and poured herself a cup of coffee. She was planning or daydreaming. The blinds opened onto the backyard. The pansies were in their beds, the roses on their trellis. It was a lark-on-the-wing snail-on-the-thorn moment until she saw the two white children from the house next door open the gate, enter our yard, head for our brightly painted swings, and settle their little fannies onto them.

Another tale from the crypt of Negro childhood. I interrupt to ask what they looked like.

"Like two white children. Nothing special. Murky blonde hair."

"Were they both girls?"

(sigh) "I think so."

Mrs. Jefferson watched as the swings began to move, then she stood and straightened her shoulders. Did her thoughts run along these lines?

The thousand injuries of Caucasians I had borne as I best could, but when they ventured upon insult I vowed revenge. You, who so well know the nature of my soul, will not suppose, however, that I gave utterance to a threat . . .

When she stepped onto the porch there was nothing urgent or harsh in her manner. "Girls," she said calmly but firmly, "Margo and Denise are taking their naps. They won't be down to play, so you can go home."

And they do. But they return the next week. And the week after that. Each time, Mrs. Jefferson steps onto the porch and speaks the same words. Each time, they leave silently. After the third visit, they come no more. And within a year they are gone forever.

A wrong is unredressed when retribution overtakes its redresser. A wrong is equally unredressed when the avenger fails to make herself felt as such to him who has done the wrong.

Now, so many years after, Mrs. Jefferson will look down, lower her voice, and end the tale thus: "I was too intimidated to confront their mother."

I can't bear to think of her intimidated. "Of course you were," I rush in. "Those police homeowners were probably still doing plainclothes duty."

Silence.

She's silent, so I try a slavery joke. "You had to watch out for the Park Manor pattyrollers." It's corny and gets a dutiful pre-laugh sound. I must do better.

"Mother, all I regret is that those people moved before we got our badminton set. That would have finished them off completely." She gives me a look that acknowledges my skill, or at least my good intentions. Then she stands up, ending the conversation, still ashamed of herself.

Mother looks stylish and confident when she drives us to school each morning. On the first day of kindergarten I fight not to be separated from her and weep with abandon. It takes two adults—Mother and the teacher, Miss Thurston—to dislodge me from the maternal body and haul me into the classroom. Within the week I've adapted, with the help of my red dress. I want to wear it each day, for a time at least, because it makes me feel brave. Mother May I? Yes, you may.

The second week I come home in triumph, mimicking a classmate who still sobs each morning. "I wanna go home to

Ma-ah-ma!" I get the three-note quiver perfect, to my parents' delight. The red dress goes back to its normal place in my well-stocked wardrobe.

We're taught coordination skills. Tumbling, bouncing two balls, one in each hand. Sometimes Miss Thurston puts us in a circle and has us wrestle two by two. Did boys and girls wrestle each other or were the contests strictly boy/boy girl/girl? What I do remember is the nervous excitement of standing in the circle watching fierce little bodies grasp and thrash each other until Miss Thurston ends the round. I know I wrestled vehemently with Judy Winter, which leaves me feeling icky and squeamish. Is this because Judy won the match? Was I embarrassed by the fierceness of my inner gladiator? Was I discomfited because I sensed that our grappling, tumbling bodies emphasized to all that we were two of four Negroes in the class?

First Grade

I play so hard at recess that I often come home with the sash of my dress ripped on one side and hanging down. The jungle gym, tag—I never know what I've done too much of to make it happen. I feel that the sash is tattling on me the way I tattle on my older sister when she overpowers me.

Each winter morning we go into the cloakroom to take off our coats, jackets, boots, and leggings. One day when we girls were already in the classroom, we heard a great stir from back there—moving feet, boys' voices, urgent *shhhhhhhhhhh*s. Our teacher, Miss Polkinghorne, a benign little round woman with white braids wrapped around her head and granny glasses, must have hurried into the cloakroom. Or sent an assistant there. For the noise stopped, and the boys were ushered into the classroom in silence. At recess one of the girls, who must have heard it from one of the boys, told us sotto voce that T. had pulled his pants down in the cloakroom. Why did he do it? Had an alpha boy like S. challenged him? T. is lively but not one of the mischievous ones I'd have picked to pull his pants down. In my mind now, though, it's he who totes the biggest boy's lunch pail to school each day. A large black-domed structure with a V in the middle, ridges on either side, and two mighty aluminum buckles.

Second Grade

I'm placed in a small advanced reading group. It's done quietly; we children understand that we are not to boast about it. Then a first-grade girl joins the group. Soon it becomes clear, though she never says so, that she hasn't just been placed in our reading group, she's been skipped to second grade. Is she smarter than the rest of us? The community learning spirit of Lab includes constant assessment of yourself and your competition.

In the fall of 1955 an important mayoral race is in progress. Who are your parents voting for, Merriam or Daley? the teacher asks one day as we sit tailor-legged in our discussion circle. Merriam Merriam Merriam, Merriam, Merriam Merriam Merriam, said classmate after classmate. Many of their parents are University of Chicago professors. Merriam is the son of a University of Chicago professor and dean. Merriam is the liberal, intellectual candidate who has criticized the relentless workings of the Democratic Party machine.

My grandmother had once been a Democratic Party precinct captain, as had Democratic Party candidate Richard J.

Daley. Daley and his Negro ally, Congressman William L. Dawson, have strong opponents in Negroland, but I've heard adult debates: Dawson is one of only two Negroes in the United States Congress, and Daley behaved well when Emmett Till was murdered. I know my parents are almost certainly voting for Daley.

The teacher gets to me. "Merriam," I say without pausing. No one else has paused. I'm sure I use my prim, obliging voice; I may even have widened my eyes slightly, and given a little smile to suggest that I knew how predictable it was. I know that a badly told lie is as bad as no lie at all.

Third Grade

Miss Randolph, who becomes Mrs. Boverman midyear, is dark-haired with a sprightly June Allyson haircut. (The ends curl up just below her ears; the bangs are side-swept.) She is lively, she is enthusiastic, and she casts me as the daughter in a play our class writes about a Hopi Indian family. I believe we showed their traditional reservation ways first, followed by their excited visit to a large midwestern city. Were we documenting cultural difference and adaptation? All that mattered to me was that I had a leading role.

Our music teacher, Miss Schoff, has curly dark hair, which she ties with a black velvet ribbon. She wears a red Chanel-style suit. We sing folk songs (what house didn't have *The Fireside Book of Folk Songs* on its piano stand?); we sing folkloric popular songs like "Jambalaya" and "Shrimp Boats Are a-Comin'"; we sing Stephen Foster songs like "Swanee River" and "Jeanie with the Light Brown Hair"; we sing spirituals. We sing "Swing Low, Sweet Chariot" slowly and softly; we let loose on "Rock-a

My Soul in the Bosom of Abraham." After that Miss Schoff has us dance to it, and after watching she singles me out for a solo in front of the class. I fling my arms out and whirl round and round in triumph.

Those of us who have siblings in the sixth grade keep close watch on their doings. Word comes down one afternoon that Denise has beaten the star boy, B., in the fifty-yard dash. Bobby says his brother Steve said that B., not Denise, won the race. Hotly, I tell him he's wrong. The boys back Steve; the girls back me. We start shouting. And suddenly Bobby and Daphne throw themselves at each other and fall to the floor punching, flailing, and scuffling. Miss Randolph has to step in before it becomes a gender riot. Denise tells me later that B. made her race three times. "Let's do it again, Denise." She kept on winning. One two three.

All third-grade classes take French with Monsieur Pillet. "Do you remember when he took a group of his students downtown to the Hilton to show us off to the MLA?" a Lab friend writes me years later. "My mother drove us." I don't remember our being shown off at the Conrad Hilton. I remember my terror as his mother drove me home afterward; at one point I could tell she wasn't sure how to get to my neighborhood. She didn't say anything, but I could tell, and I couldn't give her directions. Finally, somehow, we reached streets I recognized and I could say, "We're almost there," and thank her with an air of cheer when I got out of the car. I couldn't tell my parents I'd been afraid she'd never find our house.

Nothing highlighted our privilege more than the menace to it. Inside the race we were the self-designated aristocrats, educated, affluent, accomplished; to Caucasians we were oddities, underdogs and interlopers. White people who, like us, had manners, money, and education . . . But wait: "Like us" is presumptuous for the 1950s. Liberal whites who saw that we too had manners, money, and education lamented our caste disadvantage. Less liberal or non-liberal whites preferred not to see us in the private schools and public spaces of their choice. They had ready a bevy of slights: from skeptics the surprised glance and spare greeting; from waverers the pleasantry, eyes averted; from disdainers the direct cut. Caucasians with materially less than us were given license by Caucasians with more than them to subvert and attack our privilege.

Caucasian privilege lounged and sauntered, draped itself casually about, turned vigilant and commanding, then cunning and devious. We marveled at its tonal range, its variety, its largesse in letting its humble share the pleasures of caste with its mighty. We knew what was expected of us. Negro privilege had to be circumspect: impeccable but not arrogant; confident yet obliging; dignified, not intrusive.

Early Summer, 1956

Two Negro parents and two Negro daughters stand at a hotel desk in Atlantic City. This is the last stop on their road trip: after Montreal, Quebec City, and New York, the plan is to lounge on the beach and stroll the boardwalk. It's midday, and guests saunter through the lobby in resort wear. The Caucasian clerk in his brown uniform studies the reservation book, looking puzzled as he traces the list with his finger.

"You said Mr. and Mrs. Jefferson . . ."

"Dr. and Mrs. Jefferson," says my father.

The clerk turns the page, studies the list again, running his eyes and his index finger slowly up and down. Just before he turns it back again, he stops. "Oh, here you are, Doc. The hotel is so crowded this week. We had to change your room."

Trailing their daughters, the father and mother follow the uniformed bellboy into the elevator. It stops a few floors up; they get out; he leads them to the end of a long hall then around a corner, unlocks the door, and puts their suitcases just inside a small room, which leads into another small room. We're looking out on a parking lot.

When the bellboy leaves, our father goes into the larger small room without saying anything. He stopped talking when the clerk's finger reached the bottom of the first page. "Unpack your towels and swimsuits," our mother orders. "Read or play quietly till we go to the beach." She follows our father into the other room and shuts the door.

We unpack quickly so she won't be annoyed when she comes back. Just what is going on? All the other hotels had our reservations. Mother has said that a lot of white people don't like to call Negroes "Doctor."

At the beach we settle on our new towels and fondle the sand. Our parents, Dr. and Mrs. Jefferson, sit on their own blanket talking in low voices. Mother never swims, but our father loves to. Today, he takes us to the water's edge and watches us go in and come out.

It's getting cooler, it's late afternoon; time to fold the towels neatly, put them in the beach bag, and return to the hotel. "Take your baths," our mother says, but only after she has taken a hotel facecloth and soap bar to the lines on the bottom of the tub that don't wash away.

"Where are we going for dinner?" I ask. "What should we wear?"

"We're eating here," Mother answers.

"What about the hotel dining room?"

"We're ordering room service and eating here," she says in her implacable voice. "And we're leaving tomorrow."

Denise speaks up for both of us:

"We just got here. We didn't get to stay long at the beach. Why can't we eat in the hotel dining room?"

We resent the bad mood that has come over our parents. We want the beach and we want the boardwalk we've been promised since the trip began.

Mother pauses, then addresses herself and us. "This is a prejudiced place. What kind of service would we get in that restaurant? Look at these shabby rooms. Pretending they couldn't find the reservation. We're leaving tomorrow. And your father will tell them why."

Our father has not smiled since the four of us walked into the lobby and stood at the desk as the clerk turned us into Mr. and Mrs. Negro Nobody with their Negro children from somewhere in Niggerland.

The next morning we are told to sit on the lobby couch while our parents check out; we don't hear what our father says, or if he says anything.

We drive back to Chicago, an American family returning home from the kind of vacation successful American families have. We'd stayed at the Statler Hilton in New York and eaten in their restaurant. We'd pummeled and pounced on the bolsters of the Château Frontenac in Quebec. When Daddy asked strangers in Montreal for directions, their answers were always accurate and polite. Only Atlantic City went wrong. In the car our parents reproach themselves for not doing more research, consulting friends on the East Coast before taking the risk.

———

Such treatment encouraged privileged Negroes to see our privilege as more than justified: It was hard-won and politically righteous, a boon to the race, a source of compensatory pride, an example of what might be achieved. In the privacy of an all-Negro world, Negro privilege could lounge and saunter too, show off its accoutrements and lay down the law. Regularly denounce Caucasians, whose behavior toward us, and all dark-skinned people, proved they did not morally deserve *their* privilege. We had the moral advantage; they had the assault weapons of "great civilization" and "triumphant history." Ceaselessly, we chronicled our people's achievements. Ceaselessly, we denounced our people's failures.

Too many of us just aren't trying. No ambition. No interest in education. You don't have to turn your neighborhood into a slum just because you're poor. Negroes like that made it hard for the rest of us. They held us back. We got punished for their bad behavior.

1956, a Month After Our Trip

Professionals and small businessmen live on one end of our block. At the other end of the block is Betty Ann, somebody's daughter, we don't know whose. She has lots of short braids on her head, fastened with red, yellow, and green plastic barrettes. She wears red nail polish and keeps it on till it's nothing but tiny chips. I beg to be allowed to wear red nail polish outside, and not just when I dress up in Mother's old clothes. No, comes the answer; red nail polish on children is cheap.

In the summer Betty Ann saunters up and down the block letting the backs of her shoes flap against her heels. When she finds something ridiculous she folds her arms and goes *Oooo-oooo-OOOo, Uh-un-UNNNh.* When she laughs she bends over at the waist and shuffles her feet. Denise and I start to do this at home. "Where did you pick *that* up?" our mother asks. "Don't collapse all over yourself when you laugh."

One afternoon we see Betty Ann playing double Dutch with two girls we've never met. They laugh a lot and say *"Girrlll . . ."* Then they start to turn the ropes.

Betty Ann's the jumper. She leans in, arms bent, fists balled, gauging her point of entry. *Turn slap turn slap turn slap* and there she goes. Her knees pump, her feet quick-slap the ground, parrying the ropes till, fleet of foot and neat, she jumps out. Rapt and envious, we watch them take turns. Now Betty Ann doesn't come down to play jacks with us or borrow Denise's bike. She and her friends laugh and eat candy, and jump double Dutch. After a week of this we stroll down the block hoping they'll ask us to join. After a few days they do. Denise isn't good but she's not bad: she swings the rope correctly and manages a few solid intervals before the ropes catch her. My swinging isn't fast or steady enough, and the ropes reject my anxious feet in seconds. By the time I clamor for a third try, Betty Ann and her friends say no.

It's not the no I remember, it's their snickering scorn. I'm used to being the youngest and clumsiest when I play with Denise's friends, but if one of them mocks or reproves me, another pets me to make up for it. If they act too badly, their mothers intervene. Or Denise does, and after a short quarrel and apology they resume play.

Not now. Betty Ann's *Ooo ooh ooooo, Un-un-unhhhh* is definitive. Denise raises her voice: *We have to go home now.* Betty Ann and her friends laugh a little harder. Denise sets a slow pace, as if we're leaving by choice. My father and uncle are waiting in front of the house: they've heard the laughter and looked down the block to see us in shamed, haughty retreat. I bask in their sympathy. Over dinner the adults concur: We will never play with Betty Ann again. *She and her friends are loud and coarse. They envy you girls. We moved to this neighborhood just five years ago. We may need to move again.*

I enter fourth grade that fall. Mrs. Pollak has a pleasant, calm manner and she's our music teacher as well as our homeroom teacher. Once again we sing Stephen Foster songs and once again we sing "Swanee River." I love that song, with its octave upswing on "Swa-NEE—Riv-EEEER." One afternoon I march around the living room singing it as loudly as I had in class that day: "All the world is sad and dreary, everywhere I roam / Oh darkies! How my heart grows weary! / Far . . ."

"Margo," comes Mother's voice from the kitchen, followed swiftly by Mother herself. "What did you just sing?"

I repeat myself: "All the world is sad and dreary, everywhere I roam, / Oh dar—" She stops me flat as the *k* approaches.

"Margo, do you know what 'darkies' means?"

I do not.

"It's an ugly word about us. People don't use it anymore, but when they did, it meant the same thing as 'nigger.'"

As I take that in, Mother fumes. "Mrs. Pollak should know better. When you sang that song last year, Miss Schoff was sensitive. She changed the word to 'lordy.'"

Is it a need for thematic symmetry that makes me think this was the same year Grandma sees me playing a game in her front yard that the little white girl next door had proposed? We bend down, slump our shoulders, lower our heads to the ground, and sling rounded arms back and forth, chanting "I'se from the jungle." Suddenly my grandmother is at the screen door telling me to come inside. She informs me sternly and solemnly, "That was an ugly game. That little girl was playing it to insult you. To insult Negroes and say we are like monkeys."

These memories are as much about being humiliated by adult knowledge as about race prejudice. My mother and grandmother exposed errors I'd made. I felt humiliated in front of them. My teacher seemed to like me, but not enough to spare me a humiliating racial slur. I'd been having a fine time with the little white girl next door until we started playing "I'se from the Jungle." It's so easy for a child to feel all wrong in the eyes of adults. And when you have no idea that what you were doing is wrong . . . I hated being caught unawares. It was so dangerous, so shameful not to know what I needed to know.

Q: Why must I know? Tell me again.
A: So you won't let yourself be insulted and humiliated. So you won't let your people be insulted and humiliated.

There are so many ways to be ambushed by insult and humiliation.

All the bright young faces, generations of them, learning the standard race curriculum of wounds and grievances! The advance or demise of The Race depends on what you do, what you are, what you long to be. That was our fact, that was our fear. Will the generations that come after be at all exempt? Will they show the damage too many of us inherited?

Or acquired.

Or drove ourselves toward.

I think it's too easy to recount unhappy memories when you write about race. You bask in your own innocence. You revere your grief. You arrange your angers at their most becoming angles.

I was happy in the sanctum of that neo-Gothic elementary school. Getting out of Mother's dark red Oldsmobile each morning, climbing the wide stone steps of Blaine Hall with the other girls and boys, looking up at its spires, then entering one of three vast arched wooden doors; walking through the entrance with its stone benches, a sense of something shaded and towering in the halls our voices drifted through. It never occurred to me till I read Ruskin on Gothic architecture that this pragmatic prairie offshoot might have marked me as he said it should—affirmed that imagination was as valued as fact; appealed to the humble and the refined; celebrated arts and customs that official culture deemed rude.

We'd walk through the halls to the library, with its childhood classics and its useful learning books. Every one of Andrew Lang's colored fairy books: crimson, green, red, yellow, olive, gray, brown. Because of my piano lessons I did my duty with biographies of composers. Why do I remember Nannerl and Wolfgang Mozart so clearly as they thrilled adults with their piano playing in court after court? Handel's mother and sisters clustered joyfully around him, celebrating his first major appointment with the chant

George Frideric *Han*-del
Or-ganist and *Choi-r*-master!

Are they meant to signal a precocious feminist awareness? (Nannerl's father made her retire when she turned eighteen and marriageable. Handel's mother and sisters were just that—Handel's mother and sisters.)

Maybe they signal my early worship of child stars and my wish to be one.

I found Althea Gibson's autobiography in the library too: *I Always Wanted to Be Somebody.* Here was blunt ambition, blunt need. Which impressed and slightly embarrassed me. Her tennis triumphs were irrefutable, even though I knew Negroes were usually overpraised for sports and underpraised for art and academics. The one thing I wished she hadn't done was describe how she straightened her hair with Dixie Peach before and after matches. Why write about that? Especially Dixie Peach. The name was countrified; the oil was heavy and greasy. We used Ultra-Sheen in my family (which didn't need to be written about either).

Every sixth-grade class put on a Gilbert and Sullivan operetta. All the younger grades were invited, and if your older sibling was in one, it gave you status. Denise was Hebe in *H.M.S. Pinafore:* when the First Lord of the Admiralty declared himself "the Monarch of the Sea," she curtsied and sang, "And we are his sisters and his cousins and his aunts." Do children today find bliss in Gilbert and Sullivan? They gave us verbal dexterity and gestural finesse. We mimicked adult rituals without forgoing the rules of childhood pleasure: rhythmic certainty, sonic variety, happy endings that succeed parodic threats and dangers.

In the car on the way to school Denise read poems aloud,

swashbuckling through Victorian thumpers about carnage and dire suffering.

> *Stitch Stitch Stitch,*
> In poverty, hunger and dirt!
> And still with a voice of dolorous pitch—
> Would that its sound would reach the rich—
> She sang the song of the shirt.

I loved nonsense poetry. Mother read Lewis Carroll aloud with me, and when I was alone in the car with her I'd recite his poems. "Humpty Dumpty," "Father William," "Jabberwock," the cheerful treacheries of "The Walrus and the Carpenter." Lewis Carroll let you murder, bully, and impose your will systematically on people, animals, landscapes, and vocabularies. But Edward Lear led you into a strange, sweet world of aliens with mellifluous names and human longings.
Jumblies
Quabbles
The Yonghy Bonghy Bo
Melancholy untainted by realism.

> He weeps by the side of the ocean,
> He weeps on the top of the hill;
> He purchases pancakes and lotion,
> And chocolate shrimps from the mill.

Mother arrives home from her errands one afternoon to find Denise and me sitting on the stairs, splaying our limbs this way and that, raucous with laughter.

Listen, Mama, listen! we cry, and start to recite a poem we've just read.

> Well, son, I'll tell you:
> Life for me ain't been no crystal stair.
> It's had tacks in it,
> And splinters,
> And boards torn up,
> And places with no carpet on the floor—
> Bare.
> But all the time
> I'se been a-climbin' on,
> And reachin' landin's,
> And turnin' corners,
> And sometimes goin' in the dark
> Where there ain't been no light.
> So boy, don't you turn back.
> Don't you set down on the steps
> 'Cause you finds it's kinder hard.
> Don't you fall now—
> For I'se still goin', honey,
> I'se still climbin',
> And life for me ain't been no crystal stair.

We declaim the opening lines—"Well, son, I'll tell you: / Life for me ain't been no crystal stair"—then start to rush; we want to get quickly to the "I'se" and the dropped *g*s, to that place where "kind of" becomes "kinder" . . .

We read it like Willie Best would read it on *The Stu Erwin Show,* with wide-open mouths, gruff dips on the "I'se," and lots of tremolo.

We read it like our favorite characters on *Amos 'n Andy*—

Calhoun (Denise), the hyperactive, scheming, bloviating attorney-at-law, and Lightning (me), behind everyone's physical or mental beat with his hapless limbs, crossing eyes, and high-throated meandering syllables. Neither parent approved of the show and we were discouraged from watching. Forbidding us would only have made it more alluring.

Now we are crouched over the book acting like little picaninnies. We're surprised by the silence that meets our last, extravagant "Life for me ain't been no crystal stair."

Our mother speaks slowly so we have to sit up and pay attention.

"That is a beautiful poem and, girls, you are butchering it. You're reading it in ignorant dialect. Langston Hughes is one of our leading, best poets. This is how it should be read."

And she calls on all the resources of Negro life and history, softening the "I'se," removing the heavy downbeat on the first syllable of every verb (which makes the dropped *g* sound like a clumsy off-pitch note), lowering her voice so everything isn't mezzo forte, turning dialect to vernacular. What are parents to do, when they've taken all steps to ensure that their children flourish in the world at large, to claim their right to culture and education, when suddenly this chasm of ignorance and inferiority opens up to swallow their cultivated little selves? How did these demons of scorn and mockery find their way into your children?

When Langston Hughes taught at the Lab School for three months in 1949, he taught writing in the kindergarten, the grade school, and the high school; he taught "The Negro in Poetry" and gave two readings of his own poems.

What had happened?

Did his work leave the premises when he did, in 1949?

Was that famous poem still part of the curriculum, and were we butchering it out of embarrassment? Had we not been exposed enough at home to Negro poets? (How alien "Mother to Son" would have looked lying in the weeds outside *A Child's Garden of Verses,* which our mother read to and with us.)

. In its way segregation was a fortress. Hostile forces threatened and intruded, but life inside could be ordered. Some of our friends went to black or mostly black schools. They learned white culture inside the fortress, surrounded by versions of themselves, taught—at least sometimes—by versions of their parents and neighbors.

That was how Mother had grown up, and now we'd given her cause to brood. "When I was your age we celebrated Negro History Week. The Association for the Study of Negro Life and History was founded by Carter G. Woodson right here in Chicago. We read *The Crisis.* We were so proud when we sang 'Lift Every Voice and Sing' at assemblies and church programs."

How were those of us being naturalized into white culture to be protected without the shield of cultural segregation? How was active intellectual pride to be instilled?

From that day forward Mother began her own cultural enrichment course with evening and weekend contributions from Daddy. Though the aim was national, the focus was Chicago, with a special emphasis on friends and acquaintances.

Did you girls know that—

The U.S. Supreme Court upheld the case against restrictive covenants in housing argued by our friends Earl Dickerson and Truman Gibson on behalf of Carl Hansberry, an acquaintance and the father of Lorraine Hansberry?

Our own Provident Hospital was the first in this country

founded and run by Negroes, and the founder, Daniel Hale Williams, was the first doctor to perform successful open heart surgery?

Ida B. Wells, a civil rights activist who spearheaded campaigns against lynching, lived and worked and organized here in Chicago?

Our friend Allison Davis was the first Negro to be tenured at a major university (the University of Chicago)? He has done groundbreaking work on race and culture and the flaws of IQ testing.

The Chicago Defender was once the most powerful newspaper in Negro America? It's run by our friend Robert Sengstacke with the help of his wife, Myrtle. *Ebony, Jet,* and Johnson Publishing were started by our friend Johnny with the help of his wife, Eunice.

Our friend the Reverend Archibald Carey, of Quinn Chapel, has been an alternate delegate to the United Nations and chairman of Eisenhower's Committee on Government Employment Policy?

Black Metropolis, a major work of sociology, was written about Chicago by two Negro University of Chicago scholars, St. Clair Drake and Horace R. Cayton?

Oscar De Priest, Helen Harvey's cousin, was the first Negro elected to Congress in this century?

Katherine Dunham grew up here, got her anthropological training at the University of Chicago, and started her dance company here?

The National Association of Negro Musicians began in Chicago?

Our friend Etta Moten starred in the 1943 production of *Porgy and Bess* and sang (with dignity and skill) in *Gold Diggers of 1935* and *Flying Down to Rio*? Her husband, Claude Barnett, also a Chicagoan, founded the Associated Negro Press.

Our friend Ralph Metcalfe Sr. was an gold medalist at the 1936 Olympics?

Do you really want to know as little as your white schoolmates know about where we came from and what we've accomplished?

Fifth Grade

Miss Torrance has her hair cut like Doris Day as Babe in *The Pajama Game*. Bangs in the front, short and flat in the back. She casts me as Amahl in our class production of *Amahl and the Night Visitors*. We listen and listen to Menotti's score; we memorize it. It's like a fairy tale, with its predictably exciting flurries of drama and prettiness. We lip-synch as if lip-synching were operatic destiny. I feel none of the terror of Not Living Up, have none of the mixed feelings that in later years will make me do things like (1) throw myself down a small flight of stairs in college so I can say I've been injured and can't try out for the fencing team; (2) plunge excitedly into an essay assigned by a magazine long after I was a published writer, then withdraw, convinced that I couldn't possibly do it.

I want nothing more than to be a boy on a crutch in Bethlehem between the years 7 B.C. and 3 B.C., a boy known to tell fanciful stories, a lying boy, and why not, tending sheep alone all day with no friends, for how could the other lithe-limbed shepherd boys and girls think much of him? A boy whose mother is so poor, she must sell their sheep and send him off begging (beggars lie). A boy who struggles to be the man of the house but wants desperately to be a child whose mother is solicitous and indulgent instead of scared and impatient; a boy who hates being a cripple, who should protect his mother but can't; a boy who feels he should be exceptional and is not; a boy who tells lies not just to get attention but because he has imagination. A boy rescued by the intervention of myth; a boy recompensed by miracle.

How we work, Sandy Mentschikoff and I! She is Amahl's anguished, desperate mother, and she is amazingly expressive: a full-bodied, full-hearted parent, acquainted with grief. We're applauded, acclaimed by our classmates and their parents. It's thrilling.

I come home from the final performance with a huge blood blister on my foot, which my father takes care of. I sit in the yellow captain's chair in the den and Daddy brings his medical bag in. He pierces and sterilizes the blister. He is solicitous, impressed. He didn't leave the office to attend the performance. Still, I can see his pride as he smiles and attends to me. My talent and achievement merit his full attention.

Amahl and the Night Visitors shows on television every Christmas. We've been watching it faithfully since 1951, our pleasure taking on an ecstatic dimension when the Negro dancer Carmen de Lavallade enters as a shepherdess paying tribute to the three kings: first shy, then antic, never less than artful. Denise has first claim on her. I claim Amahl now. Chet Allen's dark eyes are huge. He has a head of curls that glow in the camera's light.

Maybe I grow flush with arrogance and pride after my Amahl triumph; maybe that's why I make a terrible mistake about friendship later that year. M. is my good friend. We take ballet classes together. (She has better feet and more grace, and she is prettier.) We both study music. (Piano for me, violin for her, though I'm considered more outstanding.) She confides to me that when her class was asked to make cutouts of themselves in profile, she had snipped off the tip of her hooked nose. And she had. The hook was gone: her profile rested demurely on the wall amid a line of straight noses.

One morning we quarrel about something and stop speaking. She tries to make it up later that day. As our classes pass in the hall, en route to or from homeroom, she leans toward me, darting out of line to whisper "Margo!" urgently, almost pleadingly. I put my nose in the air, toss my head, and walk on. I was certainly overacting. Had success aroused envy and discontent? Was I getting back at M. for having better feet and more grace in ballet class? For not wearing thick glasses and for being prettier? Soon after, I make it up with her. But I feel her reserve.

I have a sick feeling I've gone too far.

And I have. Proof will come the next year when she's courted successfully by a witty and popular new girl. And the year after that, when she accepts the attentions of the girl who'd once been my best friend.

I was good at being popular myself, though I worried about my vivacity being misread, about being thought shallow. I wrote a long piece about this in one of Miss Torrance's writing sessions (we wrote every day): I wanted it to be understood that I had a quiet, contemplative side; that I savored nature. And I feared that, saying this, I would be mocked. Miss Torrance must have read it out loud, because the class demon, a little boy named Vernon who had bangs and the hint of an English accent, informed me, his voice somber, his eyes sparkling, that he'd heard several of the kids say they planned to tease me. I was furious and mortified. I did a ten-year-old's version of a sputter.

The teases never came and Vernon never looked back. Vernon was so enviably, so confidently disruptive.

It was just around this time that my great-uncle Lucious resumed his life as a Negro.

Our Negroland friends looked as if they belonged to every group then classified as Negro, Caucasian, Asian, Latin, or Middle Eastern.

Nearly everyone at my school looked white, but that was because nearly everyone was white. Negro students were mostly varied and distinct shades of brown. My three special friends in first and second grade all looked white. But when our mothers picked us up, Carolyn's and mine traded first names and comfortable greetings. Greetings with the mothers of J. and A. held neither banter nor first names. I sometimes heard Mother telling Daddy which school mothers were genuinely courteous (A.'s mother was), which ones managed—quietly, since it was a progressive school—to ignore her, and which ones, like J.'s mother, greeted her in a way that implied they wished to ignore her.

A. and J. were definitely white. And once I started meeting Carolyn at family-friend-not-school events—a Jack and Jill party, a charity tea for Provident Hospital, dinner at the Parkway Ballroom—I realized she belonged to Negroland. My euphemisms were becoming a bit tortuous in those days. I don't remember ever saying "Negro" or "white"; I remember carefully saying "my out-of-school friends" and "my school friends"—but since some of my out-of-school friends were in school with me, this nomenclature did not serve my strategic evasions.

I was clearly maneuvering to control my racial airspace.

———

When Uncle Lucious stopped being white, my parents invited him to dinner. He had worked for decades as a traveling sales-man, making periodic contact with his sisters and with cous-ins who looked white enough to meet him in segregated places when he came to town. Then he retired, and his retirement community was Negroland.

Denise and I were told the basic story, and we greeted him politely. I watched him covertly all evening. He had the long Jefferson face. But I could find no—*no*—physical sign that he was a Negro. His nose was blade-straight, his lips sliver-thin, his skin nearly as white as his hair. I told myself, *We have friends who look as white as Uncle Lucious.* But I had always known them as Negroes. The word had kept its visual fluidity, even as it acquired social obligations and political constraints. Now I was in free fall. Who and what are "we Negroes," when so many of us could be white people? I sat there and reasoned it out: If I am related to Uncle Lucious and I am visibly Negro and Uncle Lucious is invisibly Negro and visibly white . . . Suddenly the fact of racial slippage overwhelmed me. I was excited for days after. I knew something none of my white school friends knew. It wasn't just that some of us were as good as them, even when they didn't know it. Some of us *were* them.

Our cousin Lillian Granberry Thompson looked as if her por-trait could hang in the Museum of the Confederacy. ("Lillian," she said her father always told her, "the best blood of Missis-sippi runs in your veins.") She was a few years older than my father and chose to live as a fair-skinned Negro, passing for con-venience when she wanted to patronize white-only shops and restaurants; reaping the little rewards (deference here, flattery there) often granted her by brown-skinned Negroes. She was a trusted conduit between the passers and the non-passers in Daddy's family.

So many in my parents' world had relatives who'd spent their adult lives as white people of some kind. Avocational passing was lighthearted. Shopping at whites-only stores, getting deferential service at whites-only restaurants. You came home snickering: *What fools these Nordics be!* Passing-for-life stories were melodrama prompts. P. lived as a Negro woman severed from her twin brother, who lived as a white man; N. was the only child in a family of eight to remain a Negro; H.'s brother had spent decades as a white man in a small English town; when his pass-worthy niece and I went to Europe the summer before we were college seniors, our mothers agreed that she should visit him without me. She refused to.

For the first time, Daddy told me about our cousin J.E., who'd passed as a successful white business and family man somewhere in the Midwest. I use initials to shield his public identity. His mother, my great-aunt Bessie, lived in Chicago. He would sometimes make contact with Cousin Lil when he came to town (he had risen to the top or near top of an insurance company); then she'd call other Negro relatives to set up visits. In my father's telling, the conversation was highly elliptical: "A childhood friend's in town and would like to see you—can we come by your office tonight when you've finished work?"

He even lowered his voice as he told the story. As I reconstruct it: Night has fallen. The patients have gone home, the nurse and receptionist have gone home. There's a knock on the door. Cousin Lil enters first; she and my father kiss each other's cheeks; she is followed by J.E. Do they hug or shake hands? Shake hands, I imagine, then (maybe a second's hesitation?)

trade upper-arm pats. "How you doing?" "Fine, fine. Good to see you." If it's winter, talk of Chicago's cold will get them past the first awkwardness; if it's spring or summer, the heat leads to reminiscing about their Southern childhood.

"What did you talk about?" I asked. "We talked about the old days," my father said, gazing past me. The old days, when they were all Mississippians with parents listed as "mulattoes" on the local census forms.

Why did J.E. choose to visit Daddy? Had they been especially close or was this just one visit? I didn't ask. It was as if the visit, like J.E.'s life, had to be sealed off, as if further conversation would record what must stay hidden. Daddy told me that J.E.'s white sons had gotten wind of his ancestry when he died. Was that because his wife had known or suspected? Had there been a deathbed confession? Did the boys find incriminating documents when they went through his papers? How did they find a trail that led back to Rust, the Negro college he'd attended in Mississippi before transferring to the University of M—— up north? They were thwarted at Rust, told of a fire that had destroyed a number of school records, including their father's. Was this true, or were school administrators old hands at putting white relatives off the scent of ex-Negroes? The sons persisted, somehow made their way to Chicago, where they presented themselves at their grandmother's, only to be rebuffed. How did they introduce themselves? Did they speak timidly, courteously, or gruffly and accusingly? Did they show her a photograph of the son and father who had thrown their patrimony into such doubt? I was told nothing except that she gave the answer her son would have wished. "I've never heard of that man," she said, and closed the door.

Melodrama demands a climactic tableau.

Tableau of Resolve—the Mother, defiant, preternaturally still, her voice a low telltale throb—and of Consternation: let's have one son rearing back, shocked and confounded; the other turning away, hand to chest, every muscle conveying "Thank God! I've been reprieved."

Melodrama recedes as my cousins resume their old lives or assume new ones. What had J.E. and his wife taught them about the Negro race? What did they know of Negroes before Negroness was thrust upon them? This will affect their decision. Together or apart, they can go on being white men who no longer have the privilege of taking themselves for granted. Or they can take on the touchy, hyperconscious identity of light, bright, damn-near-white Negroes. Either way, no surface will ever be superficial again.

As for Great-Aunt Bessie: she had played her part as sacrificial mother, she whose illicit standing (social, racial, sexual—choose your plot) demanded that she renounce all claims on her child. Traditional interpretations favor grief and stoic grandeur. Let's work with rage. Whatever she saw in their faces—fear, longing, confusion, disdain—Great-Aunt Bessie's sentence was her revenge. It meant "None of you can claim or disclaim me now. I don't know your father anymore and I don't know you. Whatever you want to know, I will keep hidden. And if you hope that my silence frees you to be white again, it doesn't. You've seen me, glimpsed his face in mine. You will never have a clean white slate again. You will never be able to forget that I may be the Negro grandmother who turned you away. I refused you."

All speculation. Dramatization. My great-aunt's Negro grandchildren might know more, but I still don't have the nerve to ask. I sat with Cousin Lil at Great-Aunt Bessie's funeral, and brought up the story, hoping that death would loosen her tongue. She shook her head and touched my hand, as one quiets a child about to do something inappropriate. "We're not supposed to talk about that," she said, and applied herself to conversation elsewhere.

Uncle Lucious didn't come to our house again. I have a picture of him on my father's cabin cruiser, *The Bali Ha'i*. He sits next to his sister. He looks content; she looks ebullient. My father told me that once he settled in he began to telephone his Negro relations and accuse them of neglecting him. Psychologically transparent. But he'd been a prickly white man too, said my father, regularly disturbing his own peace by getting into fights when he heard people mock or demean Negroes, as he inevitably did at the white bars and restaurants he invariably went to. "They don't talk about anything but us. What we do, how we look, how much they hate us," he told my father. But they must have talked about something else *sometime*. And the ordinary talk of ordinary white men must have been a comfort to Uncle Lucious in those early days. He could handle the nasty turns at first. Till he couldn't. Then he'd fuss and fight and make himself a target of anger. Of suspicion. So when the time came to retire, he retired, retreated, and resettled among Negroes. But he wasn't really a Negro anymore. He was a former white man. And my parents looked down on him a little. Not because he'd passed, but because he'd risen no higher than traveling salesman. If you were going to take the trouble to be white, you were supposed to do better than you could have done as a Negro.

Jack and Jill is supposed to nurture our development as the kind of Negroes who can achieve more than most white people. Jack and Jill, Majors and Minors, Trees and Twigs: national and local clubs founded by mothers to ensure that their children embody and perpetuate the values of the Negro elite.

Jack and Jill is founded in 1938 by twenty-six Philadelphia mothers, all descendants of Joseph Willson's Higher Classes of Colored Society. They display the usual Talented Tenth pride that decrees *We will continue to set high standards for the social and cultural life of our families even as white society goes on belittling or ignoring our achievements.* They are galvanized by Negroes' invigorated campaign for equal opportunities *and* advantages. They are galvanized by the liberal reformist vision of childrearing that tells them that as women they are responsible for bringing educational precision and psychological insight to the rearing of children. The influential book *Babies Are Human Beings* is published that same year.

AIMS OF THE NATIONAL ORGANIZATION

To aid in the development of a fully integrated child along educational, physical, recreational, religious, and social lines.

To aid mothers in learning more about their children by careful study.

To aid in doing something for children less fortunate than ours.

To support all national legislation aimed at bettering the condition of children.

And to display our gifts. At one Jack and Jill Christmas party, little Nicky Roberts, inordinately bright and fetching (thick curly hair, yellow-beige skin, large dark eyes), recites all fourteen verses of "The Night Before Christmas." He is at most five or six years old. The parents in the audience grow ebullient as his high voice pipes out verse after verse after verse.

I'm looking through 1950s issues of *Up the Hill,* the magazine Jack and Jill mothers produced each year. Each cover has an idyllically American drawing. In 1950 a smiling boy pushes a smiling girl in a swing attached to a flowering tree branch. (*We could be Dick and Jane.*) In 1952 a small boy and girl ride a bike together, the sky above them, trees and grass behind. (*We don't live in slums.*) The children look national-magazine-cover Caucasian.

The next year three teens in Scout uniforms clasp hands on a worthy landscape of Negro civic life: a church, a ranch-style home, and three stalwart-looking buildings present the race-progress front embodied by the NAACP, the YMCA, and the YWCA. Because the magazine cover is midnight blue and gold, there is an aura of sunlit darkness. The family on the 1956 tenth anniversary issue is Anglo-Saxon in look and dress, but dark lines have been sketched in to suggest that they are Negroes. And the 1957 cover has gone United Nations international (Dr. Ralph Bunche, one of ours, is undersecretary of political affairs at the UN, after all): images evoke each continent while youngsters of different ethnicities hold up a globe together. "The World Moves Forward on the Feet of Little Children."

What did we do, as tots, as preteens, as "Ten Pre's and a Teen," as high schoolers who called ourselves Vogues and Esquires or Shirts and Skirts? We did exactly what white American children did: arts and crafts (dolls and jewelry for girls, airplanes for boys); hayrides and sleigh rides; swim ("splash") parties, toboggan parties, tennis, horseback riding; trips to the circus, to museums, to theaters and TV studios. There were parties with puppet shows, parties with Western and Mexican themes; There was square dance and ballroom dance; there were buffets and dinner dances where "the social graces were much in evidence as the handsome young men seated the lovely young ladies at the candlelit dinner table."

I remember the Mexican-theme party because Jose R.'s mother was part Mexican and she taught us the chorus of "Cielito Lindo" in Spanish. The hayride made me feel I belonged in the jaunty Mickey Mouse Club number "Goin' on a Hayride," starring Darlene, my favorite Mouseketeer. (I feel a twinge of retaliatory satisfaction whenever I watch Nanette Fabray and an all-white cast do the dialect lines from *The Band Wagon*: "Get goin', Louisiana hayride, / Get goin', we all is ready!" they sing rakishly, and at the very end a small Negro boy in a straw hat frolics in the hay. "I is here!" he pipes.) I remember the toboggan party at a suburban ski lodge because white teenagers laughed loudly and danced unchaperoned. Maybe I'd seen previews for movies like *Blackboard Jungle*. It felt dangerously alluring.

What was especially attuned to our needs as Negroes? Social studies units that proved we had a history and cultural heritage. Philadelphia Jack and Jills learned about "the exotic island of Haiti": they made baskets, drums, and pottery, tutored by a parent who had visited the island and was "an artist in her own right," their guest speaker a distinguished "native Haitian" named Dr. Bonhomme. This was so successful, they chose to study Africa the next year, learning its history at the Schomburg Library and viewing its art at Lincoln University.

There were even ventures into integration: in 1952 the Columbus, Ohio, chapter studied Israel and Jewish culture.

The primary school children learned games and poems "that are favorites of Jewish children"; the junior high group visited a Jewish community center; the "Keen Teens" gave an interracial tea with guests from a Jewish temple.

Professional accomplishments were essential, hence the feature "Daddies in the News." Charity, too: contributions to the United Negro College Fund; Christmas toys to children in the Virgin Islands; a television set to the Boys' Club of Washington, D.C.

Here I am in the 1954 photo of the two-to-five-year-olds, wearing a jumper and a white blouse with puffed sleeves. According to the chapter's report (each chapter submitted a report to *Up the Hill*), the year began with a Halloween party: "All of the children came masked in very colorful costumes." In November we each brought a gift ("wooden puzzle, durable books or non-breakable record") for the pediatrics department at Provident Hospital, and in December our selflessness was rewarded: we brought ornaments to our own Christmas party and got presents from a grab bag. In January we "little ones" learned handicrafts; February brought Valentine's Day festivities, and March "brought folk dancing lessons to this little group." Most important, we formed a rhythm band, and rehearsed for spring Jack and Jill Day. That must have been the day that I interrupted my friend onstage with my impromptu dance.

The mothers dedicated themselves to the insights and enlightened ideals of child psychology. The Parents' Creed, "Your Child's Emotional Needs," is a model of the pedagogy and anxious self-scrutiny expected—demanded—of mothers then. A pledge of allegiance, a loyalty oath sworn to Motherhood.

Examples: The Need for Belonging ("I will develop in my child a feeling of security by avoiding extreme methods of discipline"); The Need for Achievement ("I will not try to achieve my own ambitions by forcing them on my child"); The Need for Personal Integrity in Sharing ("I will show courtesy and consideration to other people regardless of their age, sex, color, creed, or nationality").

In practical, in sociological terms, how do we reward our mothers' efforts?

Our goal, in the pledge of the Los Angeles chapter: "At the top of the hill stands COLLEGE GRADUATION and A SUCCESSFUL CAREER."

We embody the progress of a people, and not least—definitely not least—the success of its maligned family life. Our mothers advance the ongoing project of validating the Negro Woman, proving her a lady, a responsible member of her community, an exemplary wife rearing exemplary children.

For those children placed in white schools by the mother and her husband, Jack and Jill becomes a racial enrichment program, a guarantee that our social lives do not depend on the favor of white schoolmates and their parents.

At times I'm impatient with younger blacks who insist they were or would have been better off in black schools, at least from pre-K through middle school. They had, or would have had, a stronger racial and social identity, an identity cleansed of suspicion, subterfuge, confusion, euphemism, presumption, patronization, and disdain. I have no grounds for comparison. The only schools I ever went to were white schools with small numbers of Negroes.

I've always held on to some vision that at Lab, at least through fifth grade, we were free to do our childhood tasks—learn to work and play, compete, collaborate in a space largely free of race markers. No, not "free"—a space that protected us from the burdens of adult race prejudice and consciousness. To a real extent, we were. But we were not protected from our teachers. Or our parents. We were not protected from the shocks of physical difference.

"When I came to Lab in second grade, I knew I was in a foreign world," Denise told me. "The boys had bangs."

"Denise," I told her, "I've seen pictures of your Rosenwald nursery school class. More than half the kids look white."

"But none of the boys had bangs, Margo. They had curls and waves. They did not have bangs."

"Butch Dale's hair was straight enough for bangs."

"But he didn't have bangs."

We were not protected from our own fantasies. How I'd like to deny my first conscious memory of having my hair washed. I was sure, cheerfully sure, it would turn it blonde. "Get me out of this white doll / brown doll scenario!" I want to scream. "I'm better than this!"

Then I calm myself. *No one escapes her time and place. I repeat the words of my therapist: "A fantasy is a construction." I give myself a Chekhovian moment: The generations that come after will not have to endure these shaming constructions.*

Those ugly stories you overheard or were taught by parents and grandparents—these were part of the curriculum, stories that gave the lie again and again to public declarations that if Negroes would just prove themselves worthy they would be welcome as equals. Parents and grandparents told you some white people would dislike you even more if you were clearly their equal. Here were examples from their own lives and from the lives of friends.

> The University of Chicago professor who so resented a Negro graduate student's challenge that he told her, "As long as I am in this department, you will never get your master's degree." (Aunt Vera transferred to Northwestern.)
>
> The white Southern medical residents at a University of Chicago hospital who complained about a Negro doctor's being on a fellowship at all, especially when he was allowed to enter the rooms of white female patients. ("Stay by me when we go on rounds," the head doctor told my father. He did, and he completed his fellowship.)

The secret signal which one generation passes, under disguise, to the next is loathing, hatred, despair. And as a result of these, a sense of perpetual violation.

But I have to turn my mind to other things.

Because it's almost time. Whatever our race, color, or creed, my peers and I are getting ready to

> Sidle
> Slump
> Pout
> Pose
> Sashay and foot-drag
> Into adolescence.
> Devious and careless
> Feverish and slothful
> Living in the moment that's so often the wrong moment.

We'll apply Clearasil to our pimples, start biting our fingernails, learn to use Kotex, then Tampax, say things like "It's snowing down South" when a girl's slip is hanging.

I have a few years to go, but I start to get involved—half conscript, half worshipper—when Denise starts listening to *Jam with Sam* on WGES weekend nights; when she persuades our mother to drive us both to a weekend showing of *The Girl Can't Help It* ("Little Richard is excellent and Jayne Mansfield is a very good actress," we assure her when she picks us up).

Denise will whip and twirl through the house, hold on to the broom closet to practice her dance moves, stack her new 45s on the upstairs record player.

She will cha-cha to "Quiet Village" and "Poinciana," bop to "She was a foxy little mama with great big hips / Pretty long hair and pretty red lips!" She will croon, "I sit in my room looking out at the rain, / My tears are like crystal, they cover my windowpane."

I will read her discarded issues of *Polly Pigtails, Calling All Girls, Mademoiselle,* and *Mad Magazine;* likewise her copies of *Seventeenth Summer* and *Mara, Daughter of the Nile.*

She will start going to Stormy's Beauty Shop on 47th and South Park, near the Regal Theater, to get her hair straightened and styled. Mother's friends go there or to Mister Paul's. The beauticians wear pink dresses, and Stormy's glossy black bob has a cobalt blue tinge. When she complains that the hair straightener stings, she will be told, "Beauty knows no pain, Denise." The speaker is Marva Louis Spaulding, who's been married to Joe Louis and featured in *Ebony* fashion spreads. Whose beauty is beyond our feverish hopes.

With Denise I will turn away from *The Mickey Mouse Club,* where she was Doreen, the best dancer with the cutest bangs, and I was Darlene, more chipper than perky, with long braids and lead roles in Disney serials. (When competing with Doreen/ Denise was too taxing, I became little Karen, Disney's version of Flossie Bobbsey. Ringlets on her head, Cubby by her side.)

I will start watching *American Bandstand* and parrot Denise's opinion: Arlene and Kenny are the most plausible teens on this all-white show. Their hair is dark, curly, and almost greasy. They look laconic when they dance. The others don't dress with any cool, and they can't keep the beat.

Alone, I still read poetry, abandoned myself to the rhapsodies of Christina Rossetti, Sara Teasdale, and Elinor Wylie; tucked my aggressions into the discursive absurdities of "The Walrus and the Carpenter," "Father William," and "The Hunting of the Snark." Until I stumbled onto a very different poem. It was in my *Modern American Poetry*. And its first line blasted through me.

> Fat black bucks in a wine-barrel room
> Barrel-house kings, with feet unstable . . .

Revulsion/compulsion/revulsion/compulsion overcame me like the heavy beats of the broom handles of the fat black bucks who sagged and reeled and pounded on a table in a primordial Congo. From whence Negro Americans had come.

> "Boomlay, boomlay, boomlay, Boom,"
> A roaring, epic, rag-time tune

It was "The Congo," by Vachel Lindsay, and I could not turn away from it, not that day, not for days after.

> Then along that riverbank
> A thousand miles
> Tattooed cannibals danced in files
> . . . .
> And "Blood" screamed the whistles and the fifes of the
>   warriors,
> "Blood" screamed the skull-faced, lean witch-doctors,
> "Whirl ye the deadly voo-doo rattle,
> Harry the uplands,
> Steal all the cattle."

It was how newspapers and television reporters talked about the Mau Mau in Kenya—a secret society of tribal warriors who murdered whites ruthlessly, then terrorized Africans who refused to join them.

The poem's subtitle let me salvage some ironic distance: "A Study of the Negro Race." Negro scholars like Du Bois and Woodson had done serious *studies* of our race. And now, in fact just as I encountered the poem, there were two Congos, both with educated young African leaders who were demanding independence from Belgium and from France. And their quest was supported by our own Dr. Ralph Bunche, United Nations leader and Nobel Prize winner.

In my frenzied readings aloud, I made sure to heap sarcasm on the section titles. "Their Basic Savagery," I would say with scornful delight.

"Their Irrepressible High Spirits"! (Here I'd sneer.)

"The Hope of Their Religion"! (I was wearily disdainful.)

For the rest, I followed Vachel Lindsay's directions, written in the margins.

THEN I SAW THE CONGO, CREEPING THROUGH THE BLACK,	*More deliberate.*
CUTTING THROUGH THE FOREST WITH A GOLDEN TRACK.	*Solemnly chanted.*

"Be careful what you do,	*All the o sounds*
Or Mumbo-Jumbo, God of the Congo,	*very golden.*
And all of the other	*Heavy accents*
Gods of the Congo,	*very heavy.*

Mumbo-Jumbo will hoo-doo you,	*Light accents*
Mumbo-Jumbo will hoo-doo you,	*very light. Last*
Mumbo-Jumbo will hoo-doo you."	*line whispered.*

Thighbone-wielding cannibals, skull-faced witch doctors, widemouthed lowlife Negroes whooping and hollering in the streets, pig-fat Negroes prancing in red coats, doffing red top hats (why can't more of us learn to curb the love of loud colors that made white people think we're ridiculous?—how well I knew that lament).

Compulsion/revulsion / compulsion/revulsion—"Boom, kill the white men / Hoo, Hoo, Hoo." All the horrors we Negroes strove to banish from our lives and from the minds of white Americans were here, now, in my room, enfolding me in a delirium of sound and sight.

Then a confusion of loveliness. A fairyland, an ebony palace, casements of gold and ivory, jasmine-scented maidens with tiny feet and pearls in hair that I made fall to their waists in undulating waves.

The fairyland appeased me; still I fought the degrading details. Hated Lindsay for sticking elephant bone in the gold and ivory casements, for making the maidens coal-black instead of ebony. Hated him for not capitalizing "Negro."

I felt I had the tools for the last section, where "a good old negro in the slums of the town" preached piety, decried sin, beat his Bible, and set the congregation singing and testifying.

It was condescending but not vicious—not to the part of me that shared Lindsay's view of florid lower-class religion. It *was* vicious, though, when "they all repented, a thousand strong / For their stupor and savagery and sin and wrong." American Negroes were not a stuporous or savage people. That was Vachel

Lindsay's ignorant prejudice, the kind we vanquished daily through struggle, achievement, eloquent indignation. And the spirituals were a great music. I could tell he knew that despite his prejudice. For here were bits of loveliness again, a jubilee as the gray sky opened and our voices rose and pulsed to a singing wind of glory glory glory.

Then, *dying down to a penetrating terrified whisper,* the last words dragged me back.

> "Mumbo . . . Jumbo will hoo-doo you,
> Mumbo-Jumbo will hoo-doo you.
> Mumbo . . . Jumbo . . . will . . . hoo-doo . . . you."

I whispered it, I chanted it, I read it silently. I read it alone in my room and I never told anyone. My reading was furtive and excited, filled with voluptuous loathing.

I was eleven. And if pornography lures as it appalls, offers you a debased vision of yourself that some part of you yields to, then "The Congo" was my first pornography.

Sixth grade gave me proof, for the first time, that there were things I was not going to be able to win, to gleam inside of. Sixth grade offered new opportunities for uncertainty.

Not about who was smartest. That had been going on since kindergarten; we were used to that. It was the rash of new students who arrived at Lab. Most of them were a good half year older than we Lifers. Most of them came from public schools, where they'd learned worldly social ways.

They knew just who was giving off pheromones. Who was verbally fleet. Who was cute and who was hopelessly not.

I found out about the List the day I huddled with three friends for a pre-gym gossip.

D.: The boys have made a list about us.

Me: (*Singing*) "As someday it may happen that a victim must be found, I've got a little list. I've got a little list."

D.: It's who's the best looking, who has the best personality, and who's the best dancer.

Me: (*still singing, failing to get a laugh*) "And I don't think she'll be missed, I'm sure she'll not be missed."

J.: Who told you?

B.: Who's on it?

D.: Margo, you're number one in personality and dancing.

Me: I'm the lord high girl and champion. (*Sardonic to keep jealousy at bay*) Next week I'll be executed.

D.: You're number six in looks.

Me: How many are on the list?

D.: Six.

B.: Who's number one?

D.: J. and I are tied for number one.

B.: Oh, a twin set.

D.: You're number two.

B.: What about personality?

D.: (*A small pause*) J. and I are number two in personality and dancing. You're number three.

(*J. sings a few measures of "Bird Dog" and does a few dance steps.*)

Me: I don't want to go swimming today. I'm going to say I have my period.

I was a good diver. Jackknife. Swan dive. Somersault in the air. I did them all. As Mother and her friends never stopped hunting, gathering, and trading hair palliatives, we'd learned to wrap chamois cloth tightly around our heads before putting our swim caps on. I did it as quickly as possible (oh, it just helps keep my hair dry, I'd say casually when asked in the locker room). Slightly damp hair could be quashed with a brush. You lived in terror of how seriously damp hair would resist as the school day went on, rising and dulling till you got home to quell it with oil, rollers, clips, and hot comb.

S. got a crush on me that year, and he was very cute, one of the new boys, with light brown hair and a sweet perky smile. Disney boys like Tim Considine had that kind of smile. That put me in the magic circle where you talk about boys and prospects. We were in different homerooms. D. told me S. had a crush on me, and that's when I noticed he smiled at me a lot in the halls.

He was still smiling, and I was still basking, the next week when D. said, "You should feel honored that S. likes you. They don't allow Negroes in his parents' building." But it was a building in Hyde Park and Hyde Park was integrated. I lived in an all-Negro neighborhood, but plenty of my Negro friends lived in Hyde Park. I went to their houses for playdates and parties and for Jack and Jill meetings. I'd been to D.'s house too— I'd had no idea certain buildings retained their racial exclusion rights. I desperately wished a Negro friend were telling me this so we could share the exclusion.

I must have said something. I must have felt ashamed later that I'd said so little, or surely I'd remember what I said? I do know that very soon after, I stopped responding to S.'s smiles. I ignored him. I ignored him until his smiles ceased.

We were the third race. We cared for our people—we loved our people—but we refused to be held back by the lower element. We did not love white people, we did not care for most of them, but we envied them and sometimes we feared and hated them. Our daily practice was suspicion, caution at the very least. Preemptive disdain.

"Who's coming over?" my friend P.'s grandfather would ask, and if he didn't recognize the name, his face would fall slightly and his voice grow distant. "Oh, one of your little white friends."

When I was in sixth grade my mother, facing the perils of puberty on my behalf, sat me down for a talk about my white friends. *Your father and I want you to be able to compete everywhere, and we want you to be comfortable wherever you go. That's why we send you to the schools they are sent to. It's fine to enjoy the company of your white friends. But do you really think you can trust them?*

Yes, I felt that I could—I was idealistic if not altogether coherent. Yes, I felt that I could and should trust them.

Margo, wherever the white man goes, there is race prejudice. They haven't invented a test to measure that. I'm sure they won't. Maybe it's just genetic.

The Lab School combines seventh and eighth grade to produce a class of academically precocious eleven- and twelve-year-olds who are profoundly disoriented socially. We are called pre-freshmen.

"You were like little insects buzzing through the halls," an upperclassman recalled. We were nervous, we were eager, we were stranded between pre- and full-tilt adolescence. Buzz buzz buzz.

That year was, still is, a blur of striving and confusion.

Reading and rereading Agnes de Mille's *Dance to the Piper*. The need to be special projected desperately, ecstatically, onto icon after icon. Audrey Hepburn (*The Nun's Story, Funny Face*); Leslie Caron (*The Glass Slipper, An American in Paris*); Tammy Grimes (the television version of *Archy and Mehitabel*).

Watching an actor who'd come from the Goodman Theatre to our English class recite Browning's "My Last Duchess" and "Soliloquy of the Spanish Cloister." Not a day went by when I wasn't seized by the futile envy of the little Spanish monk.

> Gr-r-r—there go, my heart's abhorrence!
> Water your damned flower-pots, do!
> If hate killed men, Brother Lawrence,
> God's blood, would not mine kill you!

What I craved was a landscape on which to enact—on which to exude—the hauteur of the vengeful duke.

—E'en then would be some stooping, and I choose
Never to stoop.

I decide I will be a character actress.

At a class entertainment in Sunny Gym, I stand several feet behind M. and B. as they arrange themselves on chairs and sing "When Love Goes Wrong (Nothin' Goes Right)." It's the Marilyn Monroe and Jane Russell duet from *Gentlemen Prefer Blondes*. They don't do the vamp dance; they're more in *Gidget* mode. Pertly sad, poutily sweet. My task is to help with the last eight bars, which are sung in two-part harmony: my voice is a steadying influence on the lower part. I'm clearly visible, but I act as if I'm behind a curtain.

The Voice Speaking Choir is directed by the high school drama teacher, Sheila Belmont. She has a smoky voice and a long lean figure; she has shoulder-length blonde hair and striking hand gestures. She could be in the Beat nightclub scene in *Funny Face,* or she could play the Kay Thompson fashion editor.

She must have taught pre-freshman drama: How else would she have picked Mary and me for this prestigious high school choir?

We rehearse intensely for the concert, which will be given in Mandel Hall. (Mandel Hall isn't just for student concerts: professional musicians and actors appear there.) Our program includes group dramatic recitations, dramatizations of Eliot's "The Hollow Men," Sandburg's "Jazz Fantasia," and Hughes's "The Negro Speaks of Rivers." We do the big "River City" number from *The Music Man*. And Paul Butterfield, who's a senior, plays the kind of blues Muddy Waters and Junior Wells play in clubs not so far from where I live.

My parents go to jazz clubs and buy jazz records, though. My sister and I listen to rock and roll, not blues. Paul Butterfield reminds me that, through these hard-core rough-and-tumble bluesmen, I have access to a new kind of cultural legitimacy. White bohemian legitimacy. Beat legitimacy—Negro, white, and avant-garde.

I'm doing badly in both my social lives. My best Negro friend at Lab is a year older and a lot more socially adroit. Is she really my best friend? (Even today I love the confident tone girls use when they say "This is my best friend." I couldn't bask in that confidence; I was always competing with others for her attention. I could lose her any minute, rotate out of the light of chosen friend, hover in the shadows with other aspirants. And once there I'd see those other girls, the ones whose friendship I'd passed up for this major prize. Now it was lost to me, and they had new best friends.)

I don't have a best white friend anymore, only a constellation of good friends who are more involved with each other than with me. D. and I had such a tempestuous friendship the year before that we were exhausted: now she's pursuing M., who's also being courted by B. No one is striving to be my best friend.

So I was grateful to leave town that summer for an arts camp in pastoral northwest Michigan. Hormonal confusion and emotional desperation would be subdued by art. And that meant race could be put on hold.

Interlochen was built on what had once been Ottawa tribal

lands, between two lakes, amid towering pines. "Guiding America's Gifted Youth" was its slogan, and that firm guidance showed in the uniforms we wore: navy corduroy knickers for girls, navy corduroy pants for boys; sky-blue short-sleeved shirts of functional cotton for both. (Even Van Cliburn wore the corduroys and blue when he visited to play for us.) The socks were color-coded according to age and grade division. Mine were red.

Every hour was accounted for: classes, practice time, rehearsals, physical recreation, meals, free time. Attendance at nightly concerts was required, and we got report cards at the summer's end.

I went for three years, and I loved these eight-week reprieves from the year-round toil of adolescence. Working at art, dreaming of art, being passionate and gaily pretentious about art, being competent to good to exceptional at art—all this was a given. You were normal *and* you were outstanding. If you weren't outstanding (if you occupied one of the lesser chairs in the orchestra, or the back row of the ballet corps), you suffered, you bore it, you kept working. You aspired, and even if (secretly) you didn't, you admired those who did.

It was even normal not to have a boyfriend. The camp rules were strict—clearly it was preferable. No cross-division mixing, and scant opportunity for mixing with boys your own age. High schoolers were occasionally found making out in music practice cabins. And punished. One—a girl, I'm sure—was expelled.

The camp had been started in the late twenties by Michigan music educator Joseph Maddy, and had expanded to include art, theater, and dance. A midwestern gung-ho and up-with-people ethos remained. And by the early sixties an up-with-people conservative Republican ethos had emerged: in '62, the Chicago insurance millionaire W. Clement Stone visited and gave a go-forward-and-prosper talk based on his book *Success Through a Positive Mental Attitude* (co-authored with Napoleon Hill, author of *Think and Grow Rich*). Every camper received a copy. We high schoolers mocked him, just as we girls thwarted the dress code by wearing close-fitting sweaters without blouses underneath.

As I recall, I was one of two Negroes that first year. The other was older and much more outstanding. Darwyn Apple was a truly gifted violinist who grew up to be a member of the St. Louis Symphony (first violin section) and a respected soloist. We didn't have much to do with each other—he was older, and age divisions were strict. We exchanged the bright smiles and chipper greetings that made each of us popular. Some of my friends wished aloud that we could date.

I had my own small successes. Accepted for study with the top piano teacher, Dorsey Whittington. A drama class where I played Charlotte Brontë in a radio play. And then a near-ecstatic experience as a black housekeeper when the same drama teacher cast me as Berenice Sadie Brown, the role commandeered by Ethel Waters in *The Member of the Wedding*. Waters was in her fifties and mistress of the epically folkloric when she played it. I was a sprightly twelve. I saw nothing preposterous in this—or, rather, I refused to acknowledge the preposterousness. The same teacher had cast me as Charlotte Brontë. Maybe he'd had an impulse—ham-handed but well meant—to give me something of my own, a role that had won acclaim for a member of my race. I told myself he saw my range. Theater, I felt, was an arena where I could amend and extend myself by inhabiting not pure sound, but other identities.

A honey-haired camper named Lauren played Frankie to my Berenice. Her cabin was opposite mine, so we rehearsed fre-

quently and vehemently. I'd seen the movie on television. I'd
seen Julie Harris in those lofty Hallmark Hall of Fame productions too, playing Anouilh's ecstatic Joan of Arc, and playing a
sensitive Irish nun whose faith was challenged by death, war, and
patriotism versus desire. Of course I craved all her high-voiced
intensities and oddities. But that was impossible. So I grasped
for the stoic and epic. I'd seen Ethel Waters in *Pinky* too. You
didn't think of Faulkner's "They endured" when Waters was
on-screen. *She* endured, she made everyone notice it, and she
made some pay for it. *Member of the Wedding*'s script had turns
and textures never given to those other Negro stalwarts of the
screen, Hattie McDaniel and Louise Beavers. But it wasn't only
the script; it was Waters. She did more than watch and react to
the white characters; you watched her think about them and
about herself. Sometimes revising her responses according to *her*
needs, *her* mood. I didn't even mind her weight.

I was trying to enter a world tied to my history but not my
autobiography. It stirred me mightily and it was beyond my ken.
In that way I probably wasn't much different from those white
kids my age struggling to play blues for the first time. Did my
"deep blues" accent sound any better than theirs? ("Honey, I
just don't understand that," I said, shaking my head in stoic
woe.) I think it's fair to answer *Probably not*. I think it's fair to
say *No*. Paul Butterfield's accent had sounded better.

University High: 1960–1964: There's no help for it, this girl is going to be unhappy for a good three of the next four years. One of so many unhappy high schoolers, each with their own sphere of fact and trouble (a phrase I found years later in William James).

Those of us who've been together since kindergarten, since first, second, third grade, are intimidated by the new arrivals. Jews and Negroes draw the most notice, especially Jews. The newly arrived Jews are Big Ten and Preppy Types: he with trim slacks and button-down shirts, striding through the halls; she with mohair sweaters and matching skirts, well-tended flips and pageboys; all with their fraternities and sororities, not allowed at U-High, but talked about, known about. Both had friends in public schools. Cool, daring friends.

The newly arrived Negroes are much fewer in number and much less influential overall. The boys cut a style-swath, though, importing snappy black talk. They saunter-swagger, even in their Henry Higgins sweaters, their button-down shirts and straight-legged pants. The girls are much quieter; most girls can't get away with such street flash. (The one who does is treated like a facsimile boy. She parries the smart guy-talk with no sign of intimidation. Which leads, by senior year, to hints that she's as fast sexually as she is verbally.)

What both groups signify—openly, blatantly—is the power of those who are not WASPs to exclude and include. The Jews are better at it, of course. There are more of them and they are white. Still a minority group, though, and—this is what's so enviable, so alluring—a minority group with the power to set the standard others have to envy, imitate, rebel against, or recede before.

A FEW SPHERES OF FACT AND TROUBLE

—Interracial dating, unless you were an out-and-out Beat who listened to Studs Terkel's radio show; played Mose Allison and *Missa Luba;* sneaked into blues and jazz clubs.

—Being designated "creepy." Small groups of cool boys would gather in the stairwell and let you know what they thought.

—Wanting to be distinguished—smart and talented— without alienating anyone. Wanting to be ubiquitous and popular.

I crave the gift of recreational shallowness. The trick of knowing when to be cleverly trivial, lightweight; when to avoid emotional excess.

What else did this craven, anxious high school "I" want?

I wanted to make cheerleading again and again. For, miraculously, I had made the squad freshman year, the only freshman to do so. A pure merit decision, it must have been, for I had vivacity but no particular style credibility or prestige.

Oh, the ashen rewards of merit.

Those bus rides to games, where I wasn't pointedly ignored, just easily overlooked.

Practice sessions with the other cheerleaders, all with sanctified good looks and status, all sophomores or upperclassmen. They were perfectly pleasant, and that perfect pleasantness, void of any cruelty, was just what showed I didn't belong.

Everyone was white that year, true, but the active cruelty came from my own: the girl I considered my best friend took me aside to imitate the imitation G. did of me on the gym floor in my thick glasses: waving my hands in rhythm, doing the split victory jump, with one of those head-moving blank smiles Little Stevie Wonder had.

Which didn't stop me from trying out the next year. And failing. Trying out the year after that. Failing again, outstripped by classmates who'd never thought they could make it till I did.

There must be something beyond all this twaddle! An intellectual interlude, for instance.

We, the students of Audrey Borth's sophomore English class, are being ardently well educated, studying great and good British and American writers, being readied for initiation into an adult We of critics, scholars, and uncommon common readers. This year we will read essays—comely yet challenging essays—by E. M. Forster, George Orwell, and James Baldwin.

A smaller We, Baldwin and I, have privileged relations. We are both Negroes; we are both intellectual. He is a serious, famous artist; I long to be seriously artistic and famous. I am at an advantage in this class, as I was not when we read Mark Twain as freshmen.

My mother has stocked our library with classics. I read *Tom Sawyer* and *Huckleberry Finn* in childhood, moved listlessly on to *Kidnapped* and *Treasure Island*, then left them, unfinished, to the older sister who proclaimed herself the hero of every adventure and doubled as the smarter villains too. I was a jealous little she-reader; I resented pouring myself into the lives of hero-boys.

I did my duty in the classroom. I was a good student. But Huck was not of my ilk. Cheeky, scene-stealing, Southern-white-trash antebellum boy. And what was to be done with Nigger Jim, that man-by-stealth slave, discharging his duties as boy-playmate? He was an object lesson in slavery's wrongs. How could he be an imaginary companion for me, daughter of We, the Negro elite, who never stopped asking aggrieved rhetorical questions like "Why is it always the Nigger Jims who show up in Mark Twain's fiction? Why couldn't he base a character on Warner Thornton McGuinn, the first Negro graduate of Yale Law School?" Twain actually met McGuinn and was so impressed he offered him financial aid the same year he published *Huckleberry Finn*. But he never made it into a novel. We are not what They want to see in their books and movies. Our We is too much like Theirs. Which threatens them, bores them, or both.

But now here we are, white and black students both, reading the Negro James Baldwin. And here I am at home, upstairs by myself, reading him and preparing for class. What do my white friends think as they read? What will we say in class tomorrow, and what measure of engaged detachment will I bring to our and their discussion?

I pick up the book and turn to the assigned essay.

Notes of a Native Son
By James Baldwin
"Many Thousands Gone"

The story of the Negro in America is the story of America—or, more precisely, it is the story of Americans. It is not a very pretty story: the story of a people is never very pretty. The Negro in America, gloomily referred to as that shadow which lies athwart our national life, is far more than that. He is a series of shadows, self-created, intertwining, which now we helplessly battle.

Who is this "We"? It's you, white readers. But what of We, his smaller band of Negro readers? His Negro in America is the Negro that so many Negroes like me dread having plural relations with.

One may say that the Negro in America does not really exist except in the darkness of our minds.

"One": a pronoun even more adroitly insidious than "we." An "I" made ubiquitous "Our": say it slowly, voluptuously. Baldwin has coupled and merged us in syntactical miscegenation.

We Negro readers will pause here and arrange ourselves in attitudes of easy triumph. We are throwing off that "helplessly" which Baldwin initially placed on us. We are anything but helpless now, as he unfurls clauses, vaults across semicolons, submits ignorance to rigor and unreason to stringent passion.

Close the book. (Breathe deeply.) James Baldwin is proclaiming right of entry with every possessive pronoun, integrating America by means of grammar and syntax. No demonstrators hosed into the air and crashing onto pavements, no tear-gassed bodies coughing and twisting, no children your age dressed in exhaustively clean, pressed clothes to walk shielded by armed guards into schools built to deny them.

The ways in which the Negro has affected the American psychology are betrayed in our popular culture and in our morality; in our estrangement from him is the depth of our estrangement from ourselves . . .

The Negro Baldwin has inserted himself into your life, white reader: this "our" claims all you possess. You thought you were just reading him—no, you are living with him and all of his relatives now, and if you flee you will find yourself resettled on a despoiled patch of psychic land, where you will live in severely reduced circumstances. You will be estranged from the only You worth having. You will have no privileges my We is bound to respect.

I can't sit still anymore. I move from my desk to the couch in the next room, but curling up with pillows feels childish. I need to be upright and vigilant as I read. I go back to my desk.

We cannot ask: what do we really feel about him? What we really feel about him is involved with all that we feel about . . . ourselves.

And it's a good thing I'm upright and at the ready. I know all too well what We think of this potent, deviant Negro: he threatens the achievements of My Negroes each time we make another dignified incursion into American life. I want to renounce that shame and contempt now, join Baldwin to construct a complex, compound Negro We.

When I reach the essay's end, I feel adventuresome and daring. He is so proud yet vulnerable, so full of longing and righteous hauteur. He has what I want, and I read on, follow as he summers in an obscure Swiss village ("This world is white no longer, and it will never be white again"); scores his own *American in Paris,* orchestrating Africans, Algerians, and Frenchmen in counterpoint; makes his father a Lear on Harlem's heath, himself the Edgar who lives to take the measure of a changed world.

Finally I approach the shabby unhallowed ground of the first essay. "Everybody's Protest Novel," Baldwin calls it, and "Everybody" is anybody who has ever written a socially conscious book maimed by *shrill outbursts* and *thin exhortations*.

The Mother of this unseemly brood is Harriet Beecher Stowe. I haven't read the lady, and I don't need to—everybody's educated Negro has been sick and tired of her book since the final years of the preceding century.

I settle myself on Baldwin's arm and we sally forth. Together we execute a gleeful double cabriole:

Uncle Tom's Cabin is a very bad novel, having, in its self-righteous, virtuous sentimentality . . .

I fumble, falter; I can see the words that follow. I straighten up, try to match his gait once more.

. . . having, in its self-righteous, virtuous sentimentality . . .

I stutter-step—for here comes the damning conclusion:

. . . having, in its self-righteous, virtuous sentimentality, much in common with *Little Women*.

Oh no, not that. Must I throw off the *Little Women* of my girlhood? The *Little Women* of We Happy Two, my sister and me, with our petticoats and patent leather shoes, our music and dance lessons, our diaries, our parties, our unceasing instruction in manners and morals. Girls whose utterly benign father is often away from home doing good for his people—Captain March: Dr. Jefferson. Girls whose Marmee—our Mother—pours and settles herself into every space of their being.

Baldwin's scorn is majestic. Sentimentalists like Louisa May Alcott do not truly feel, he scoffs; they play at feeling with *fluttering outbursts* that show just how much they fear the stuff of real life, real experience.

In the end he doesn't condescend to give them their own pronoun. In the end, the only sentimentalist truly worth his scorn is the one who exposes *his* fear of death, *his* arid heart.

Silly lady novelists. Silly girl readers.

My future beckons. I can renounce all shallow girl tastes, striving ceaselessly to be a Negro Intellectual like Baldwin, as good as or better than any white He. Or I can become an exemplary Teacher and Mother, one who will pass her love of literature, serious and sentimental, on to the children in her care.

I close the book, go to the couch, and lie down.

That summer was my third and last Interlochen respite. I decided to major in drama as well as piano. My reward was being cast in *The Taming of the Shrew* as Grumio, Petruchio's punning, silly yet shrewd manservant. Gender freed up; servant status unchanged—and enhanced by race, I now realize: American traditionalism in this piece of nontraditional casting. I did enjoy Grumio's impertinence toward his master: "Why, give him gold enough and marry him to a puppet or an aglet-baby, or an old trot with ne'er a tooth in her head, though she has as many diseases as two and fifty horses. Why, nothing comes amiss, so money comes withal."

I wore tulle and wings to be in the chorus of *Iolanthe*. ("We are dainty little fairies, ever singing, ever dancing / We indulge in our vagaries in a manner most entrancing.") I decided to be bold about getting through eight weeks of summer without a beauty shop appointment. I used my straightening comb openly, almost jauntily, and as I'd hoped, several white girls with curly to frizzy hair started using it. In Chicago, we knew which white girls had to get their hair straightened in Negro neighborhoods; we'd see them, and snicker about it behind their backs. But this was cheerful and conspiratorial. Without shame on either side.

On the last day of camp, prizes were given out, just before we girls went through the ritual of falling into each other's arms in tears to the finale of Liszt's *Les Préludes*. I won Honor Camper to applause and cheers. I had done everything right in front of everyone in sight. I was Interlochen's Miss Congeniality.

That was the summer another Negro girl had appeared in navy knickers and the light blue knee socks of the high school division. There'd been a second boy too, a clarinetist, but this was the first Other Girl. We passed each other on a pine-sheltered path, and I assessed her as we stopped to exchange greetings. She wore glasses (I had contact lenses by then), and I thought I heard a slight Southern accent. I knew I wasn't altogether pleased to see her. Which shamed me. I could hear my parents when they talked dismissively of Negroes who refused to acknowledge other Negroes in public with the polite nod and murmured greeting that conveyed "Good for us both. Good luck to you." "So insecure," my parents would mock. "So desperate to be the Only Ones." My words to her were dutiful and minimal.

Do you have to be here? I was thinking.

Parents and families arrived the final weekend to enjoy the

concerts and take us home. That's when someone's younger sister, a girl no more than seven or eight, approached me at The Well, the camp center where we loitered, chattered, and bought sweets.

"Excuse me," she said, clearly excited, "but are you starring in a show on Broadway now?"

It was 1962. Diahann Carroll was starring in *No Strings* on Broadway. Something in me went almost mad with excitement at the thought of anyone, even a small, gullible white girl, thinking I looked like Diahann Carroll, saucy, confident, playing a top model in Paris, with her even, rounded features, recognizably Negro, appealingly not intrusively Negro. (So encouraging, that.) Carroll had claimed the dream space once occupied by Lena, Dorothy, and Eartha.

I smiled graciously. "Why no," I said, as if speaking to a young fan. "You must mean Diahann Carroll. She's in *No Strings* and she's wonderful." Then, head high, shoulders back, I strode on. Ludicrous, yes, and what cared I? I'd been a tween Ethel Waters and that was real-time ludicrous. This was the stuff of my dreams.

That Yeats line, "In dreams begin responsibilities"? At Interlochen dream responsibilities were my respite from real ones.

And when I come home, my parents have moved us to Hyde Park–Kenwood. "My father was so excited—he said, 'This shows the neighborhood's improving,'" my white friend J. tells me jubilantly. Are my parents excited? If so, they mute it to pleased and satisfied. For some years now they've looked askance at some of our newer, rougher Park Manor neighbors. They've wanted a more socially stable neighborhood. They're touchy, though, about seeming too eager to live among white people, as if that were a good in itself. We have Negro friends there. Those in real estate, whose job is to abet Hyde Park's strategies for socially stable integration, arranged the move.

My parents are pleased with the excitement of J.'s father, though. He's in one of the more liberal organizations that, since the 1940s, have proposed, amended, negotiated, and legislated housing acts and redevelopment plans that will ensure Hyde Park remains the intellectually, economically, socially, and culturally desirable neighborhood it has been since the nineteenth century; that it will reflect the prestige of its overlord, the University of Chicago. Each organization—each committee, board, commission, council, league, corporation—has its particular constituents. Each has its sphere of law and politics, ethics, and expediency.

With some variations in tone and approach, their de facto and de jure goals have been

> to remove low-income Negroes who lived there;
> to prevent low-income Negroes from moving there;
> to convince large numbers of upper-middle-class whites to
> > remain there;
> to permit small numbers of upper-middle-class Negroes to
> > move there.

The essential question, as posed by one organization's president in a private note to a liberal alderman: "How do you tell desirable from undesirable Negroes?"

The university's chancellor offered one answer in his address to the desirable Negroes of the Kappa Alpha Psi fraternity: Hyde Park whites must look for Negroes with "similar tastes and standards."

Income. Profession. Manners. With organizations continuing to monitor just which buildings, streets, and enclaves were suitable for these controlled experiments in integration.

We live in one of two three-floor condominium buildings at 50th and Woodlawn. Everyone there is a family friend or acquaintance. Everyone there is a Negro.

We live across the street from the largely but not wholly white enclave of Madison Park, where J., her sister, and her parents live. In a year I'll watch the Beatles on *Ed Sullivan* at their house, and burst into tears when Sidney Poitier wins an Oscar for *Lilies of the Field*.

The new apartment is one floor instead of two, but it's capacious. I admire its wood-paneled dining room, its solarium, the Arts and Crafts iron grating on the heavy entrance doors of the building.

I'm starting my junior year. I can walk home from school now, or take a short bus ride.

How did I get home before this? How did most of Lab's non–Hyde Park Negro students get home through the years? When we were old enough to take public transportation, we gathered in small groups and journeyed across the Midway, that expanse of green where our gym classes played soccer, lacrosse, and field hockey; the Midway, whose 220 yards separate the university from the Negro neighborhood of Woodlawn; the Midway, which, in raucous contrast to the neoclassic glories of the White City, housed the faux-ethnographic exotica of the 1893 World's Fair. There, visitors gaped at the lower stages of civilization on display in a hastily built Streets of Cairo, an Eskimo village, an Algerian, a Dahomean, a Chinese, and a Javanese village, a Hindu and a Santa Fe Indian village, all with imported or facsimile natives, all enhanced by mongrel entertainments—juggling, magic, belly dancing, ragtime— and by the techno-carnival wonder of the Ferris wheel spinning in the sky above.

So we, Lab's Negroes, would leave the White City of Lab, cross the Midway, and take one or, usually, two buses to our faux-exotic homes in the ethnographic settlements of Bronzeville, Park Manor, and Chatham.

Now I belong to Hyde Park with its tasteful polygot past: the upper-class and upper-middle-class residents who built or moved into fine large houses (some with droppable architect names like Burnham, Baldwin, and Wright); charming smaller houses (some of them, too, with prominent architect imprimaturs); its familiar ethnic and religious progression of settler WASPs (and a smattering of Catholics), followed by Jews, followed by Asian, Hispanic, and Negro Others. The wealthy, the prosperous, the respectably struggling; professionals, scholars, artists, and political activists. Students reading, talking, smoking avidly in bookstores and in Steinway's drugstore; eating Polynesian at the Tropical Hut; lounging in cafés and offbeat design shops; going to the Hyde Park Theater, where I saw my first foreign films.

Hyde Park has always known how to make its citizens feel that their daring is, at bottom, stable. Reassuring. That they earned it by standing firm against suburban blandishments and choosing the urban way. That they—we—have the bragging rights of pioneers, even as we savor the comforts pioneers always provide their descendants with.

So here I am, walking home, past Frank Lloyd Wright's Robie

House, thinking of things both serious and shallow or chatting away with friends. If it's junior year, I'm still preppy in matching skirts and mohair sweaters. If it's senior year, I've moved toward bohemian-fetching—nylons with my penny loafers instead of Adler socks, a black A-line skirt and top, a Greek bag my sister brought me from Kitty Hass in Cambridge, Massachusetts.

I'm in the zone. Just in time for my senior year I make cheer-leading again. At last. I'm voted captain and we practice over the summer, sometimes ferried back and forth in Stefanie's red MG (her parents' red MG?—no matter), top down, sunglasses on. At the first pep rally in September we five burst through the open doors of Sunny Gym, maroon skirts swinging, maroon and white pom-poms undulating. The crowd claps and whoops as we begin our choreographed call-and-response:

> Well, hi, gang! *(Well, hi, gang!)*
> Well, what are we here for? *(What are we here for?)*
> We're here to win! *(We're here to win!)*
> Well, who says so? *(Well, who says so?)*
> Well, Ev-ry-bod-y! *(Well, Ev-ry-body!)*

Let's look at this from a third-person perspective. It will impose, or at least suggest, more intellectual and emotional control.

Senior year she will triumph with straight As—proof, her proud and rather chagrined parents note, that she could have done that all along. When she becomes cheerleading captain, she will join the select ranks of Negro girls so rewarded. (Call the roll: Jean Han-cock, sister of Herbie; Candace "Candy" Love; Dorothy "Dottie"

Fleming; Nancy Gist.) She will be asked to play the piano at the senior prom. She will play Debussy's "La Cathédrale Engloutie," not very well because she refused to practice enough in advance. She still loves the idea of being an actress, and she does have a role, not a lead, a secondary role, in the senior play. It's Pygmalion. *The drama teacher, who is temperamental and charismatic, will explain production procedures and note that, in casting, he will look for as much physical symmetry as possible. She waits for those fateful seconds a well-timed comic response needs, then she offers the schlep's quick shrug, hands open, palms out. She gets the group laugh. "That was very good," says the drama teacher, shaking his head; he looks merry and approving, as if she'd just responded to his direction with the perfect improvised bit. She is cast as Mrs. Pearce, the housekeeper.*

Decades later, when she is a published writer, that drama teacher will leave a message on her answering machine. Is she the same Margo Jefferson, and if so would she call him back? But if not (he sounds a little timid, a little anxious), he's sorry for the intrusion. She could call back and take her revenge by delivering some calm truths about his fits of temper, which now look like self-important pique, not artistic rigor. She could remind him of that ruthless moment when he made it so very clear that she would not be cast as Henry Higgins's clever mother. Why say it aloud and expose her in front of everyone? Why not simply cast her as Mrs. Pearce instead? He must have known in his small heart that she deserved to be Mrs. Higgins.

She doesn't call back. That's my revenge, she decides. He's been reading me; he's intimidated; his anxious voice gave him away; his need to call gave him away.

There's always subtext, though. She deserved to be Mrs. Higgins, but she did not deserve to be Eliza. Not incorrectly, he thought her friend M. the more talented. If she attacked now, would he retaliate with that?

She still sees herself offering—improvising—that comic gesture, the deflating bit of humor that makes an audience feel "Oh thank you for not making us uncomfortable, for letting us feel we're better than the truth the joke reveals." Humor is being ingratiating when you're afraid to be aggressive.

Here was her character flaw. (Not a tragic flaw—we're in the realm of bourgeois drama.) She wanted to belong in too many places: she couldn't make herself be a rebel, a designated outsider. Is this why she still had no reliable best friend, just pleasing flurries of friendship with girls who were already taken? And were there racial distinctions to be parsed here? With her white friends, there wasn't all the room for boy talk, and party talk—they weren't going to the same parties most of the time or seeing boys of the same race. They weren't going to each other's houses regularly after school or on weekends. With Negro girls, her style wasn't top of the line. The deftly held, fully inhaled cigarette at parties; the easy verbal byplay. She was too eager and earnest. She lacked that touch of remoteness, of teasing froideur. She didn't deliver cutting-edge slang effectively. (Watch her practice "Mellow-spoo—doo" in her room after hearing Angela say it in a bid whist game. It has to be light, almost languid. Try not to overdo the last syllable. Watch her work "You must be on DOPE" into a phone conversation—it conveys mocking disbelief—and feel idiotic when her mother emerges from the kitchen to ask "Do you know what that means?") When she turns thirteen, friends arrange a party for her birthday. Even as they chant "Surprise!" and she gasps and smiles and gives a girlish squeal, she feels cheated. You didn't really want to give me a party, *she thinks.* You wanted a reason to give a party that your parents would like.

BOYS

When she ponders it, the decline begins in sixth grade when she's voted as having the most personality, being the least good-looking. A decision made by Caucasian boys, with one Negro most likely participating.

She wasn't doing particularly well with most of her own in those days, though José Randall did give her a card and a box of candy for Valentine's Day. (Why couldn't she hold on to that, use it to enhance her sense of her appeal?)

At a Christmas party pre-freshman year, even though she's wearing too childish a dress (her long-sleeved princess-line deep-green velvet with the lace collar, clearly wrong because L. doesn't compliment her), L. does hear several of the boys in their sisters' crowd remark that Margo's going to have a really good figure.

Why didn't she hold on to that? Why blame her glasses for everything? True, they provided a few ninth-grade setbacks: P.W., the cool, sexy boy she got a crush on, is calling her "Blind," amiably, almost fondly, not harshly, so the other boys feel comfortable following his lead.

But B.G. had a crush on her—they met at a party in August, when she'd come back from her first summer at an arts camp, still wearing her glasses. B.G. was Sullivan's friend, and they were both public school boys. L. was very excited about Sullivan, and B.G. was coming to U-High in the fall. When a group of them went to Riverview a few weeks later, he kissed her in the Tunnel of Love. She was politely inert.

L. had explained "grinding" to her: on a slow record, the boy would press his stomach into yours and . . . grind . . . and you would grind lightly if you wished in response. (If an unwanted partner got too insistent, you pulled away and left his pelvis to push and circle air.)

"We do at parties what you do on dates," we'd tell our white friends. (They started dating freshman year; we hadn't.) But she— that she is still me—did as little as possible. All through high school she would get violent crushes on people but be unable to return their overtures. When handsome R. asked her to go with him sophomore year, she said yes, then returned his ring after a scant week. Senior year G.H. asked her to go with him as they sat in his parents' car after a Nancy Wilson concert at Ravinia. Her answer (amiable, not harsh): "Why don't we keep it platonic?" So ended what had begun three years before when he imitated her on the gym floor, cheering in her glasses like Little Stevie Wonder.

Senior year is the year of J.L., keen-featured and lustrously dark, expert at playing the street boy, the gouster. Expert at toying with three girls in our Negro set, serious girls, each of them, and all the more enthralled for that. This is hopeless, *she thought.* I can't trust him to want me for myself. *Which self would that be, miss? she might well have asked—but at least G.H., sharp-tongued and a touch jaded, liked her humor. J.L. gave no such sign. Their attraction was fairly generic. She was vivacious and hard to get with a good figure. He was the acme of Negro Male Cool. They'd grown up together. Been in Jack and Jill together. His mother and her father practiced medicine together.*

And they had absolutely no way to grasp each other's spheres of fact, trouble, and longing.

———

Edwin L. Jefferson, Ronald Nelson Jefferson,
and Ruby Cozette Jefferson, 1908. The family lived
in Coffeeville, Mississippi, but the photograph
was probably taken in Jackson.

Irma James Armstrong and her mother,
Lillian McClendon Armstrong, in Chicago, c. 1920.
The photograph was for relatives in St. Louis,
who'd sent Irma the handsome but too-big coat.

Irma, photographed by Gordon Parks, 1940–41. Parks was working at the South Side Community Art Center as its official photographer and learning his craft alongside such artists as Charles White and Margaret Goss Burroughs. Marva Louis, the model and wife of Joe Louis, had seen Parks's fashion photography in Minneapolis and offered to help find him work if he moved to Chicago.

Bernard Jefferson and Ronald Jefferson
with their band instruments in Los Angeles, c. 1922.

Irma and Ronald, just engaged,
in Los Angeles, 1941.

United States Army Captain Ronald Jefferson
at the all-Negro base in Fort Huachuca, Arizona, c. 1944.
He was in the army from 1942 to 1946.

Irma and Ronald with their daughter Denise
in their Bronzeville, Chicago, apartment, c. 1946.

Margo Jefferson,
c. 1950.

Denise reflecting and reflecting
on her image, c. 1951.

Margo and Denise in Boston, during the
family's cross-country trip, c. 1956.

Irma hosting a New Year's Eve party in a mandarin Chinese jacket
and with a Claudette Colbert bob, c. 1956.

U-High's varsity cheerleaders.
Co-captain Margo is in the back row, center, 1964.

MARGO JEFFERSON
Be glad and your friends are many.
                                        Anonymous
French Club . . . Cheerleader . . . Junior
Class Treasurer.

Margo's high school
yearbook photo, 1964.

The years 1963 and '64 were years of integration experiments. Earlier a few of us had been invited to bar and bat mitzvahs, even to occasional evening parties. But for non-bohemians, the basic out-of-school parameters were: boys roughhouse and do sports together; girls shop and go to plays, movies, and museums together. There's a brief plan, rumor has it, to extend limited fraternity membership to three U-High Negroes; give them athletic but not social privileges. The plan is quashed, rumor has it, because fraternity members at public schools raise the possibility (the threat) of recruiting lower-class Negro boys with high athletic skills.

Girls act with more discretion. Sleepovers are largely out of bounds. Birthday parties are usually fine. We're most comfortable without our parents. Mine have a cabin cruiser docked on Lake Michigan, and we often visit the boats of our Negro friends. When we see white schoolmates and their parents on the lake, we all wave with scrupulous cheer and move on. Visits are out of the question. Neither set of parents wants the social strain. They're supposed to be relaxing, not working.

We do our best to turn that strain into stylish adventure. Major political changes lead to minor social changes. Minor and shallow but still worth noting.

The time: 1963.

The place: A meeting of the Etta Quettes, one of my all-Negro girls' clubs. Two of us asked the other members if we could invite a few (just a few) white friends to the autumn party. They voted yes.

We chose girls who'd been our friends for years. We trusted their style: they were cute; they were quick-witted; they could dance, even to songs that hadn't found their way onto white record charts. We knew their parents were progressive. We knew they knew Negroes were cool, that it was daring and flattering to be invited to one of our parties. We knew they'd factor all this in when they chose their dates.

Every one of them did well. They looked good. They danced nicely and unobtrusively. They didn't gawk or try to draw attention to themselves.

And they talked about it for days afterwards. They were thrilled to be there.

Wherever I was, whatever I did, I wanted to be popular. I was considered talented; I was inclined to be intellectual. I valued both. When they brought me praise, I valued them; when they made me feel too eccentric, I edged away. Being popular in all worlds would steady the course between Exceptional and Irreproachable. Make up for the price talent and brains might ask of me. Banish the specter of being handicapped by race. Twice over: among whites, and among Negroes who found me—let me put it very precisely—socially inept due to an excess of white-derived manners and interests.

Miscalculation on all fronts. Though I could manage it often enough and well enough, the quest killed brain cells and confidence for years. I didn't see how paltry it was. But I did know it was tenuous.

What I would have to do later, starting in college and in the years following, to become a person of inner consequence: break that fawning inner self into pieces.

THE BOX

Here is a box, in which I shall place/put the personal material of my college years. Four years, a foursquare box.

And outside the box, the tumultuous world.

Within the box, four years of internal hopelessness, a squeezing into my perceived limitations and deficiencies.
   Not talented enough.
   Not brilliant enough.
   Not an exceptional personality.
   Fated to be that contemptible girl thing, a dilettante.

1964

Hoping for a kind of extracurricular Advanced Placement, I tried out for cheerleading, made it, and realized almost instantly that I'd attached myself to a perky ethos that wasn't respected. Intellectuals were respected, bohemians were respected, art was respected, serious angst was respected.

Modes of Manhattan chic, from Fifth Avenue to Greenwich Village, were respected.

I tried out for the drama society and won a part in Genet's *The Maids.* I played Madame, the shallow, gilded object of the maids' murderous desire, and I felt shallow, faced with the talent and experience of the other two actresses. I knew cheerleading had been a fateful mistake at an early rehearsal when the older actress said, "Margo, you made cheerleading, congratulations"—it was in the school newspaper—while her tone said, "I won't be rude about it, but we're making art here, and you're a throwback to midwestern Americana." I dragged my pom-poms and my synchronized cheers through one basketball season and never mentioned the episode again.

When I showed a flair for fencing in gym (left-handed and sure-footed from all that ballet), the instructor asked me to try out for the team. I wasn't interested, but I couldn't say no when teachers or parents asked me to do something flattering and ostensibly reasonable: How could one say no without stirring up disappointment and reproofs I had no answers for?

I found other ways of preferring not to: in this case I practiced falling down a half flight of stairs in the dorm, and when I inflicted a small bump on one leg, I put a bandage on it, limped to the gym the day of the tryouts, and claimed to have a knee injury.

1966

I did get to play a maid onstage, though she lacked all of Genet's feral glory. I was a warm, loving Negro American maid in a musical based on *Suzuki Beane,* a bubbly beatnik alternative to *Eloise.* This was the last thing I wanted to do—no middle-class Negro, brought up to wince and sigh whenever Hattie McDaniel or Louise Beavers appeared on camera, wanted to play this role. We MCNs used to trade "me-and-the-maid" tales from visits to white friends. At times me-and-the-maid gave each other quick looks: I'm proud of you, said hers; we are still one people, said mine. At times the maid avoided my eyes and was more attentive to the white guests, whereupon I displayed my ease among them. Sometimes we were trapped together, as on the night in college when a group of theater students gathered around the host's piano at a party in Weston, Massachusetts. We were singing show tunes and I was taking a turn as accompanist. As we rolled into the Gershwin songbook, our host stopped suddenly, saying "Wait—you have to hear this," and rushed into the kitchen. Moments later he returned, followed by the maid, who was still wiping her hands on her apron. He led her to the piano, let her arrange herself, and turned back to me.

"Play 'Summertime,'" he said. Then, to the now-silent group around the piano, "Listen to this beautiful voice."

Did the maid and I exchange a look (my usual claim) or did we avoid each other's eyes? (More likely, since all eyes were upon us.) Did she have a beautiful voice? I know it was adequate. And I know she and I did perform "Summertime." I believe there was uncertain applause. Not everyone was as obtuse as the host, but everyone was trapped by his hospitality.

It was time I spoke out and spoke up. I told the director I had serious reservations, since Negro maids were generally stereotypes. "No no no," he said. "Of course they are. This is not that at all. She's a dignified woman. And you'll get a good song." So I gave in to my greed to be onstage again and my eagerness not to appear touchy. And got stuck singing a ballad called "There's More to Life Than You'll Ever Know," cradling a gamine my own age whom the audience justly found adorable.

Gr-r-r—there go, my heart's abhorrence!

And then . . . And THENNNNNNNNNNN, as the Coasters intone, facing mock disaster . . .

I failed to get a good role in a British play whose title I now refuse to recall. I was sure I'd get it; I'd been the only Negro in the drama group freshman year and I'd done well in *The Maids*. But I was a mannered, sardonic actor (all the more reason I should never have been cradling Suzuki Beane), and the part called for edge and emotional attack.

I was so furious and mortified that I never auditioned for another college production.

No wonder that when Black Power came along the next year I used it as an excuse to stop talking to various people I felt hadn't respected or acknowledged me enough. Who said the personal always had to be *honorably* political?

I was trying to be honorable in my political reading, my political opinions, my modest actions against the Vietnam War and for Black Power. It wasn't hard to try—everyone around me was trying.

Senior year I found my way to a Boston theater group, one of so many experimental groups reading Artaud and Grotowski; following Joseph Chaikin, Richard Schechner, Ellen Stewart, and Joe Papp; trying out techniques and rituals borrowed from Asia, Africa, Latin America. We did a piece called "Riot" in which a panel discussion among three types (an earnest white liberal, a black nationalist, a cautious moderator) was encroached upon by images of street disorder (a rat on a trash can, a mixed couple making love) and finally the images exploded into a full-scale riot—or insurrection—battering the audience with strobe lights, sirens, running bodies (rioters and police) that froze, at intervals, into attitudes of struggle, anger, and terror.

Civil rights.

Anti-war.

Black Power.

Feminism and gay rights heading our way.

The luck of being born close enough to a right time in history! However miserable you were personally, whatever the follies and failures of each movement, they made you think about the world. They gave your feelings an objective correlative. They made you try to think beyond the self you took for granted.

Where was that ingratiating little integrationist in high school who listened quietly, letting only regret cross her face, when S. took her aside to explain that she couldn't be invited to P.'s party because P.'s Southern parents didn't approve of social integration between boys and girls.

Where was the little snob, en route with her best Negro friend to a Gilbert and Sullivan rehearsal for *Utopia, Limited,* who stood over a stoop-shouldered ghetto girl just before her bus stop and said, "You need to shave your legs," and, as the girl looked up and said, "Thank you," ran down the bus steps giggling.

It became necessary to take blunt weapons to whole parts of oneself and hack away.

This is how I talked then, smashing and hacking away.

Well, of course the ghettos are going up in flames—the last Good Nigger is dead. I did respect Martin Luther King, but his death proves that nonviolence is irrelevant. (I have nothing but contempt for Thurgood Marshall—he supports Johnson on the war. The media wants to call them riots, but they're uprisings. Why should black people behave well to get their rights? White people don't behave and they get all the rights they want. That's been our mistake as privileged Negroes. Believing all that "We have to be twice as good to be acknowledged just as good. Everything we do must reflect well on the race."

We take on white people's ridiculous pretensions and they make us look even more ridiculous. Mother said this herself from her position of bourgeois privilege. She told my sister before her senior year in high school, "Now, you can come out next year, or you can go to Europe." And as soon as Denise's reservations were booked, she added: "What are Negroes coming out into anyway?"

Mother used to say, "Most white people want to see us as just more Negroes."

That's exactly what we need to be—Just More Negroes. We need to take strength from that. Give what we have and what we know to the community.

Who are we? Who do we love? The summer Uncle Archie came North and passed for white so he could work at RR Donnelley and earn money for law school, he missed Negroes so much he would sneak over to the South Side on weekends and go from stand to stand getting his shoes shined. All afternoon getting his shoes shined. Give him a few drinks and he's telling jokes about a Shreveport Negro so pig-ugly everyone calls him Oink. Then he puts his baseball cap on backwards and says, "Let's play, 'Nigger.'"

Mother and her friends loved to joke about our Afros.

"You know, Margo," she drawled at one of her afternoon luncheons, "if a fly got caught in there, he would break his little wings trying to get out."

They need to re-examine their lives. They have a lot to answer for.

In Negroland boys learned early how to die. They started in their teens, dying in period rec rooms with wood paneling and pool tables, train sets, golf clubs, liquor cabinets.

Did Father keep a rifle on the wall there, or did the son find his old army gun in the bedroom closet and sneak it downstairs? There, in the rec room, an amiable, well-mannered doctor's son shot himself. Motive, unknown; verdict, accidental death; time, not long after his father was arrested for assaulting his second wife.

A few years later, in another rec room, a sweet-faced doctor's son with a soft voice did the same. Suspected motive: he feared going the way of his father, sweet-faced, soft-voiced, seductively effusive, and (suspiciously) no longer married.

Vietnam opened other routes to self-extinction. A Negro boy could drop out of college, enlist, and come home a junkie. He could drink, shoot up, steal for several years, pawn his grandmother's silver, assault a homeless man, and evade a jail sentence because his parents, both doctors, knew the judge. He could retire to the family homestead in Virginia, decline steadily in health, and die of kidney failure.

Negroland children were warned by their parents that few Negroes enjoyed their privilege or plenty; that most non-Negro Americans would be glad to see their kind of Negro returned to indigence, deference, and subservience.

Their parents made sure to supply them with well-appointed homes and apartments, tasteful clothes and plenty of them, handsome cars, generous allowances, sailboats, summer camps, music and dance lessons, flying lessons, private schools, tutors, and an array of clubs where other children exactly like them met for sports and directed play, cultural excursions, and Christmas visits to old people's homes to sing carols.

Nevertheless, life in Negroland meant that any conversation could be taken over by the White Man at any moment. He dominated dinner party army stories about the brown-skinned Negro officer who'd had to escort his angry unit to the shabby back cars of a segregated train; the light-skinned Negro officer who'd been given the last seat in the white section of a train until he said he was a Negro, whereupon a porter (another brown-skinned Negro) was sent to find a curtain that could separate him from the Caucasian in front and join him to the Negro behind.

When he's not lynching you, he's humiliating you, said the men at the dinner table. They leaned forward and raised their voices, then subsided into their chairs, shook their heads, let out a *hmmnnnn. He keeps you out of his hospitals, his law firms, his universities. Even his damn cemeteries. He never lets you forget you're a second-class citizen.*

Strategic privilege and flagrantly displayed prosperity let you forget. Cocktail parties and dinner dances urged you to forget. Season tickets to the opera, summer trips to the Caribbean and Mexico. The family together watching *Ed Sullivan,* watching *Gunsmoke* and *Maverick,* watching *Playhouse 90* and outstanding cultural productions like *Peter Pan* and *The Nutcracker.*

Suavely complicated marriages and urbane extramarital liaisons; hushed quarrels at the breakfast table. Fathers at the office, at the club, coming home late so many nights.

Mothers picking the children up from school, shopping, planning meals, lunching with friends, working to safeguard their marriages.

La Vie Bourgeoise.

Round up the usual Oedipal conflicts and divided loyalties. Fathers, insist that your sons become high-achieving Negroes, prepared, like you, to push their way manfully past every obstacle.

How are they to do this? Force of will. You did.

But the boys had started dying.

Negroland girls couldn't die outright. We had to plot and circle our way toward death, pretend we were after something else, like being ladylike, being popular, being loved. Between the late 1940s and the early 1960s, Good Negro Girls mastered the rigorous vocabulary of femininity. Gloves, handkerchiefs, pocketbooks for each occasion. Good diction for all occasions; skin care (no ashy knees or elbows); hair cultivation (a ceaseless round of treatments to eradicate the bushy and nappy). Manners to please grandparents and quell the doubts of any white strangers loitering to observe your behavior in schools, stores, and restaurants.

We were busy being pert, chic, cool—but not fast. Fast meant social extermination by degrees, because the boys who'd sampled a fast girl would tell another girl they'd taken up with (who was desirable but not fast) that the first girl was a slut.

The boys knew this because she'd made the mistake of being fast with more than one boy, so they'd talked about her with each other.

And then her girlfriends talked about her with each other. They were still cordial to her at parties. She wasn't put out of her clubs. But if she wasn't already in the Etta Quettes or the Co-Ettes, she wasn't asked in.

Occasionally, a daughter who'd been silly enough to get herself pregnant would actually drop out of college, have the child, and marry its father. That meant she had disgraced herself and her family.

In fact, she had committed matricide: she had destroyed the good reputation her mother, her grandmothers, and her grandmothers' grandmothers had fought for since slavery.

Premature sexual activity and pregnancy out of wedlock? She was just another statistic to be held against the race.

The world had to upend itself before shades of possibility between decorum and disgrace could emerge. Suddenly, people like us were denouncing war and imperialism, discarding the strategic protocol of civil rights for the combat aggression of Black Power. We unmade our straightened hair, remade our pristine diction, renounced our social niceties and snobberies.

The entitlements of Negroland were no longer *relevant*.

We were not the best that had been known and thought in black life and history. We were a corruption of The Race, a wrongful deviation. We'd let ourselves become tools of oppression in the black community. We'd settled for a desiccated white facsimile and abandoned a vital black culture. Striving to prove we could master the rubric of white civilization that had never for a moment thought us the best of anything in their life or history.

You grilled yourself: Do I still like—love—too many white writers, musicians, artists? Have I immersed myself enough in African history and culture? Do my principles show in my work? And principles notwithstanding, in my heart am I still a snob? At meetings, in political conversations, class—your *back-ground,* your *advantages*—weasels its way in. Purge it from your intellectual pronouncements; it pops up in how you expressed them. The preemptory tone that you tell yourself is rigorous. The way of seeming to listen politely when you aren't listening because you are so sure you know better.

And even when you didn't think you knew better, you'd get those looks at community poetry readings or concerts, once a nationalist heard your diction or watched your mannerisms . . . watched until you felt his gaze and had to return it; then he'd slowly curl his lip.

And the comments:

You have to understand: you can't be trusted. You've always insulted people like me.

Yeah, you Chicago folks' Scotch budget could fund a year's research at the Institute of the Black World.

When the Revolution comes, people like you will be lined up against the wall and shot.

Are you black enough became essential to style preening and sexual intimidation.

Good Negro Girls in search of lives their parents hadn't lived often sought men their parents didn't know and didn't care to know.

Naturally, errors were made. The doctor's daughter study-ing architecture married a man with suspected ties to the drug trade: within the year, she was shot in the head from behind and left beside her murdered husband, a large pool of blood widening in what *Jet* magazine called their "affluent South Side home."

The dark-skinned daughter of a socially responsible educator, who left her Paris career as a provocatively keen-featured model with exorbitant long limbs to teach early childhood education at an Illinois community college, was stabbed multiple times in the head and neck by an estranged husband who then drove her body to the police station and turned himself in, telling the officer, "I just went crazy."

Average American women were killed like this every day. But we weren't raised to be average women; we were raised to be better than most women of either race. White women, our mothers reminded us pointedly, could afford more of these casualties. There were more of them, weren't there?

There were always more white people. There were so few of us, and it had cost so much to construct us. Why were we dying?

The first of the dying boys had succumbed to the usual perils of family life—the unkind, philandering father, the kind but closeted father, the absent or insufficient mother. After them came the boys who threw off privilege and lusted for street life, imitating the slipslide walks of the guys who lounged on street corners in caps and leather coats, practicing the raucous five-stage laugh (clap, fold at the waist, run forward, arms in loose boxing position, squat, and return to loose standing position); working as hard as any white boy at a frat party to sound like Bo Diddley and Otis Redding.

Striving ardently to be what they were and were not. Behold the Race Flaneur: the bourgeois rebel who goes slumming, and finds not just adventure but the objective correlative for his secret despair.

I won't absolve the girls. We played ghetto too, rolled and cut our eyes to show disdain, smacked our gum and loud-talked.

But the boys ruled. We were just aspiring adornments, and how could it be otherwise? The Negro man was at the center of the culture's race obsessions. The Negro woman was on the shabby fringes. She had moments if she was in show business, of course; we craved the erotic command of Tina Turner, the arch insolence of Diana Ross, the melismatic authenticity of Aretha.

But in life, when a Good Negro Girl attached herself to a ghetto boy hoping to go street and compensate for her bourgeois privilege, if she didn't get killed with or by him, she usually lived to become a socially disdained, financially disabled black woman destined to produce at least one baby she would have to care for alone.

What was the matter with us? Were we plagued by some monstrous need, some vestigial longing to plunge back into the abyss Negroes had been consigned to for centuries?

Was this some variant of survivor guilt?

No, that phrase is too generic. I'd call it the guilty confusion of those who were raised to defiantly accept their entitlement. To be more than survivors, to be victors who knew that victory was as much a threat as failure, and could be turned against them at any moment.

I'm still obsessed with James Weldon Johnson's 1933 diagnosis of this condition. It deserves repeating.

Awaiting each colored child are cramping limitations and buttressed obstacles in addition to those that must be met by youth in general. How judicious he is. Yet, implacably, this dilemma approaches suffering, *in exact proportion to the parent's knowledge of these conditions, and the child's ignorance of them. Some parents try to spare their children this bitter knowledge as long as possible. Less sensitive parents (those maimed by their own bitterness) drive it into the child from infancy on.*

At each turn, Johnson forgoes high rhetorical drama. He chooses "this dilemma" over "our burden," prefers our "condition" to our "fate," and comes at last, with stately tread, to this: *And no parent may definitely say which is the wiser course, for either of them may lead to spiritual disaster for the child.* Tragedy has arrived and is content to wait quietly. In time it may be able to claim both parent and child.

Those of us who avoided disaster encountered life's usual rewards and pleasures, obstacles and limitations. If we still had some longing for death, we had to make it compatible with this new pattern of living.

In the late 1970s, I began to actively cultivate a desire to kill myself. I was, at that time, a successful professional in my chosen field of journalism. I was also a passionate feminist who refused to admit any contradiction between, on the one hand, her commitment to fighting the oppression of women and, on the other, her belief that feminism would let her draft a death commensurate with social achievement and political awareness.

A little background is needed here. The women's movement was controversial in the black community at this time. Many men and all too many women denounced feminism as a white woman's thing, an indulgence, even an assertion of privilege, since she was competing (and stridently) for the limited share of benefits white men had just begun to grant non-whites.

Black feminists responded that, thanks to sexism, women of color regularly got double blasts of discrimination and oppression. And, anyway, we had our own feminist history. Relations between white and black women had been wary, inequitable, or bluntly exploitative. Alliances between them had been scant and fraught.

Nevertheless, social and cultural progress through the decades had made interracial cooperation and friendship available to my generation. I'd had white friends since kindergarten. And I was willing to acknowledge this irony: the rituals of bourgeois femininity had given the girls of Negroland certain protections the boys lacked.

That vision of feral, fascinating black manhood possessed Americans of every race and class. If you were a successful upper-middle-class Negro girl in the 1950s and '60s, you were, in practice and imagination, a white Protestant upper-middle-class girl. Young, good-looking white women were the most desirable creatures in the world. It was hard not to want to imitate them; it was highly toxic too, as we would learn.

Still, these rituals allowed girls the latitude to go about their studies while being pert and popular, to stay well-mannered and socially adaptable, even as they joined the protests of the sixties and seventies.

So, when the black movement and the women's movement offered new social and cultural opportunities, we were ready to accept them.

But one white female privilege had always been withheld from the girls of Negroland. Aside from the privilege of actually being white, they had been denied the privilege of freely yielding to depression, of flaunting neurosis as a mark of social and psychic complexity. A privilege that was glorified in the literature of white female suffering and resistance. A privilege Good Negro Girls had been denied by our history of duty, obligation, and discipline. Because our people had endured horrors and prevailed, even triumphed, their descendants should be too strong and too proud for such behavior. We were to be ladies, responsible Negro women, and indomitable Black Women. We were not to be depressed or unduly high-strung; we were not to have nervous collapses. We had a legacy. We were too strong for that.

I craved the right to turn my face to the wall, to create a death commensurate with bourgeois achievement, political awareness, and aesthetically compelling feminine despair. My first forays in this direction were petty. I conducted my own small battle of the books, purging my library of stalwart, valorous titles by black women and replacing them, wherever possible, with morbid, truculent ones by my sisters. Out with *This Child's Gonna Live,* up with *There's Nothing I Own That I Want.* Goodbye *My Lord, What a Morning* by Marian Anderson; hello *Everything and Nothing* by Dorothy Dandridge. As for Mari Evans's iconic sixties poem,

> I am a black woman
> . . . .
> strong
> beyond all definition still
> defying place
> and time
> and circumstance
> assailed
> impervious
> indestructible
> Look
> on me and be
> renewed

I tore it out of an anthology and set fire to it in the bathroom sink.

I found literary idols in Adrienne Kennedy, Nella Larsen, and Ntozake Shange, writers who'd dared to locate a sanctioned, forbidden space between white vulnerability and black invincibility.

A Negro girl could never be purely innocent. The vengeful Race Fairy always lurked nearby; your parents' best hope was that the fairy would show up at someone else's feast and punish *their* child. Parents had to protect themselves too, and protect you from knowing how much danger you all were in.

And so arose one variation on the classic Freudian primal scene in which the child sees or imagines her parents having sex and finds it stirringly violent. Here the child sees and imagines her parents having fraught encounters with white people who invade their conversation and shadow their lives beyond the boundaries of home or neighborhood.

Work hard, child. Internalize the figures of your mother, your father, your parents (one omnipotent double-gendered personage). Internalize The Race. Internalize both races. Then internalize the contradictions. Teach your psyche to adapt its solo life to a group obbligato. Or else let it abandon any impulse toward independence and hurtle toward a feverishly perfect representation of your people.

The first unapologetic black female suicide took place in a small Off-Broadway theater in 1964, in a short Gothic play by a fiercely imaginative Negro woman playwright. I wasn't there, but I understood that Adrienne Kennedy's *Funnyhouse of a Negro* was as much a demand for freedom as the Civil Rights Act passed the same year.

Kennedy's heroine, Negro-Sarah, is a young middle-class woman, *good-looking in a boring way; no glaring Negroid features, medium nose, medium mouth and pale yellow skin. My one defect is that I have a head of frizzy hair, unmistakably Negro kinky hair . . .* She lives alone in an Upper West Side brownstone, longs to be bohemian and distinctive, fears she is merely drab and decorous. She mistrusts her white poet boyfriend: *he is very interested in Negroes.* She mistrusts her own passion for white culture. Its great works have no place for her; its great figures would deem her an insignificant cultural arriviste. One woman, one room, one anguished, polyphonic consciousness. Queen Victoria and the Duchess of Hapsburg prowl her psyche, lamenting the awful curse of blackness. Patrice Lumumba and a shadowy black father are there too; they struggle and fail to lift that curse. At the play's end, the light goes black, then blazes white. "The poor bitch has hung herself," says the landlady. "She was a funny little liar," adds the boyfriend.

Negro-Sarah embodies our Negroland legacy of proscription and privilege, grief and achievement, a mingled love and shame for our people, a mingled love and terror of white culture. And then (as if the result of these others), despair and a furious will to extinguish the self. My people's enemies have done this to me. But so have my own loved ones. My enemies took too much. My loved ones asked too much.

Let me say with care that the blame is not symmetrical: my enemies *forced* my loved ones to ask too much of me.

Nella Larsen's 1920s novels were republished in the late 1960s and early '70s, part of an exuberant rush of books by women, by gays, by non-whites of every hue, that the culture had contentedly left out of print for years. Some of these books appeared in pleasing well-wrought editions. Larsen's were among those given the cheapest paper and crudest design publishers could get away with. Her own heroines would have disdained to buy them.

For they are touchy and proud, these Jazz Age heroines. They read widely, wear soigné frocks, give smart parties, and make clever remarks. They have keen minds, keen features, and fair skin, and can be suitably ironic about "what called itself Negro society." They cultivate the advantages of being New Negroes and New Women; sometimes they even indulge in being New Negroes who can pass for white. They pursue La Vie Bourgeoise with too much anxiety or too much ambivalence. Their sexual allure trips them up; their sexual reserve holds them back. They are timid where they should be bold, reckless when diplomacy is needed. Secretly, they feel contempt for their own failure to imagine anything more for themselves.

Each one finds death of some kind: a lethal marriage, a fatal accident. But their longing for death, the drive toward it, is never quite acknowledged. Larsen's women stumble into suicide by misadventure or miscalculation. They avoid premeditation, just as they avoid stringent self-reflection.

So, when Ntozake Shange stood on the stage of the Public Theater in 1975 and spoke the words "And this is for colored girls who have considered suicide," my heart took flight. We were the same age. We were both doctors' daughters who'd attacked our girlhood gentility with the weapons of Black Power and radical feminism. Now we could consider—toy with, ponder, contemplate—suicide.

I tried to quash my envy by seeing the play two, three, and four times, taking friends and paying for their tickets. I told myself, *Ntozake is laying the groundwork for all black feminists. She's taken her stand as an artist, while you hide behind being a journalist. You must rid yourself of jealousy. You hate the second-raters who quibble with the brave ones.* I'd always derided Anne Sexton's suicide competitions with Sylvia Plath. "Thief!" Sexton wrote, "how did you crawl into, / crawl down alone / into the death I wanted so badly and for so long . . . ?" *Maybe because Plath had more nerve and wrote better poetry* was my answer.

I channeled my envy into aesthetic dissatisfaction with the words that followed. "For colored girls who have considered suicide when the rainbow is enuf." It wasn't enough. It was "For colored girls who are moving to the end of their personal rainbows." I found the rainbow overused and trite, even if it was an honored symbol in every culture, a sanctioned trope of lyric poetry. When I'd finished this spiteful formalist critique, I was left alone with my fury. Ntozake said we had found god in ourselves and loved her fiercely. I hadn't and I didn't.

I wrote bleak notebook entries and called them death aphorisms.

I loathe my kind, which is humankind. We maim and taint whatever we encounter. We might improve but I don't think so.

I think more people should kill themselves. What incentives can we offer?

Freud got so much credit for saying "civilizations have death wishes." I say individuals have life sentences, and I refuse to be a model prisoner. I shall consider my death an evolutionary advance for the species.

I wrote to the Hemlock Society for instructions. Thirty aspirins minimum, with a liquid that makes you drowsy. Then tie the plastic bag over your head.

I studied suicide notes. It's a primitive genre—they all follow the same basic pattern. "I can't go on." "I'm so sorry to do this to you." "You've been so good to me." "You've been as good as anyone who doesn't have to go through anything like this can be."

I kept a folder of my drafts. Sample: "Dear _____: I won't go on. I've known everything was hopeless for a long time. Why keep fighting?" This prose is nothing to write home about—but it's homeward bound, isn't it? Add your own personal touch. I always put in something about who my jewelry should go to.

I knew I should have an alternative method, and I chose the oven. I liked its literary pedigree—from *Hansel and Gretel* to Sylvia Plath. When I actually tried putting my head in it, I realized that the oven opens about a foot from the floor, so you have to twist your body around and put your head on the door at a weird, forced angle.

I practiced because I did not want to be found in an ugly sprawl or a fetal position. I started at five minutes and worked my way up to fifteen. *One of these days,* I pledged, *I'll have the courage to turn the oven on.*

I knew that unrequited death is as futile as unrequited love. *You must take hold,* I told myself. *You are suffering the long-term effects of profound fatigue. This is the result of all the work, the years of work required to be wholly normal and wholly exceptional. You must set an example for other Negroland girls who suffer the same way.*

You must give them a death they can live up to.

Practice, practice, practice. Like playing scales, taking a barre. Do your daily suicide warm-ups.

There were journal entries, naturally.

Sample 1

Listening to Billie Holiday sing "You don't know what love is / Until you've learned the meaning of the blues," I think, *You don't know what unrequited love is till you've loved a culture that doesn't love you back.* Call my album *Torching with the Token.*

Sample 2

Dying to be impeccable
    And merely dying instead.
    Why didn't you respond directly to words that hurt and belittled you?
    By seeming not to mind I'd show I was a good person. They'd feel my goodness and be ashamed. They'd have a conversion experience on the spot and never be prejudiced again.
    I cry your mercy, pity, love—ay love!

Every day a little death
Suck it up.

There were quotes culled from women writers, black and white deliberately juxtaposed.

A sense of incalculable past loss and injury, and a dread of incalculable future loss and injury . . .
   (Fanny Kemble, 1852, after conversing with the slaves on her husband's Georgia plantation)

I do not approve of swaddling oneself in the griefs of ancestors who suffered infinitely more than we. And yet, I lived like this long before I found these words.

I think this journal will be disadvantageous for me, for I spend my time now like a spider spinning my own entrails . . .
   (Mary Boykin Chesnut, 1860, considering her own state of mind on a South Carolina plantation, as she manages home, husband, slaves, and social duties)

This is a way to show my self-aware double consciousness: I descend from the belittled and despised; I descend from the rewarded too. This begins as a racial division, then becomes a class division, in which a sense of loss, injury, grief, becomes the possession of those with time to articulate it attractively. Unhappiness as an avocation.

———

I had wanted to compromise with Fate: to escape occasional great agonies by submitting to a whole life of privations and small pains. Fate would not be so pacified . . .

"But if I feel, may I *never* express?"

"Never!" declared Reason.

I groaned under her bitter sternness. . . . If I have obeyed her it has chiefly been with the obedience of fear, not of love.

(Charlotte Brontë, *Villette*)

Fear, resignation, and then, as respite, Jane Austen's "desolate tranquility," lying on your couch for hours, face turned to the wall, listening to music, renouncing ambition, taking long afternoon naps.

I sometimes wish that I could fall into a Rip Van Winkle sleep and awake with the blest belief of that little Topsy that I never was born . . .

(Harriet Jacobs, considering her state of mind, as, having at last won freedom from slavery, she labors over the book that will become *Incidents in the Life of a Slave Girl*)

Oh to flee consciousness, to be extinguished at last! To stop telling oneself, I do this for my people.

You are you and you are going to be *you* forever. It was like coasting downhill, this thought, only much much worse, and it quickly smashed into a tree. *Why was I a human being?*

(Elizabeth Bishop, "The Country Mouse")

I completely agree, which is why I've never had children.

———

My hand is stuffed with mode, design, device.

But I lack access to my proper stone.

(Gwendolyn Brooks, *The Womanhood:* "The Children of the Poor")

Despite being given every advantage. Your despair is self-indulgent.

Plunge ahead, put one foot in front of the other, straighten your back and your shoulders and everything else that is likely to slump, buck up and go forward, and in this way, every obstacle, be it physical or only imagined, falls face down in obeisance and in absolute defeat, for to plunge ahead and buck up will always conquer adversity: so Mrs. Sweet's mother had said to her when she was a child . . . for her child—the young Mrs. Sweet—needed to have drummed into her very being the cli-chéd words of the victorious.

(Jamaica Kincaid, *See Now Then*)

The meaning beneath her mother's words is terror—terror and fury at having to be afraid. It's not that her clichés are false. It's that they deny, cover up emotions that would tell the child what she truly needed to know.

I have stories to tell?

I have cuts and bruises that do not map a course.

(Wendy Walters, "A Letter from the Hunted in Retrospect")

And none of them are justified unless you find a way to make the story worth telling.

There were bleak little exchanges with like-minded black friends.

Dialogue 1

—I've been reading Rachel Carson. *Lost Woods.* Environmentalism contains a vision of human extinction. Let me away from here to spend my days "in the drifting community of the plankton, in the midst of diatoms, dinoflagellates, and other microscopic plants; in the company of minute crustaceans, worms, peteropods, and hosts of other larvae."

—I heard a story on NPR this morning. A peacock wandered into a Burger King parking lot. Customers were feeding it Whopper fragments and wilting fries when a Negro man suddenly appeared in their midst and began to beat the peacock. It was a vampire, he shouted, and beat the bird until most of its tail feathers were gone. When the animal rescue people arrived, they had to euthanize the peacock. The police arrived soon after to remove the shouting man. His fate is unknown.

Dialogue 2

—The women of our generation weren't well trained in the narratives of the male workplace. Fucking and fighting, pissing and kissing.

—We're learning. I've just been in a pissing contest with an associate.

—Did you win?

—I will. Now I know it doesn't have to be bigger, it just has to piss farther.

Dialogue 3

—I have no job at the moment. I do have a house with a mortgage payment I can just meet. I quote James Brown to myself: *Money won't change you but time will take you on.*

—Do you think those were his wife's last words before she died on the plastic surgeon's operating table?

—Or did she think *Why didn't I marry that nice Ike Turner?*

Parting Monologue

—I've never been so sick of RACE in my life.

If I have to talk about RACE and its subdivisions—ethnicity, culture, religion—any more, I will do a Rumpelstiltskin. I will stamp my foot and disappear into the earth.

Every group with its rights and grievances, its mathematically precise litany of what has been denied, what should have been granted long ago, what must be restored and redressed. Even everyday WASPs compete now. Because their sense of being dispossessed, displaced, bullied, has in an amazingly short time become as acute, as outraged, as righteous as that of the groups they managed and mangled for so long.

—This is my dream. Eradicate them all. Then fix your hair, and put your hands in your muff as your heels go clip clip clip across the pavement.

—*May I help you, ma'am?*

—*Thank you, sir, I've just murdered quite a few people and I need a taxi.*

Looking back, I think my mother's words "Sometimes I almost forget I'm a Negro" had came back to me in a new and contentious idiom. With external failure out of the question, internal discord seemed the only protest mode. A temper tantrum I could permit myself. My own private register of what had been forbidden.

Forbidden by the Negro Clubwoman, our foremother, apostle of achievement and discipline. "Be stalwart and virtuous," she urged. "Use your education and your manners to advance your people's cause and prove your value to society. To prove that our women deserve the utmost respect. Never let anyone guess you have selfish, wild thoughts. Never show weakness. And remember: you are as honorable as any white woman, and you have had to work much harder for your honor."

She founded service organizations, lobbied for social and political rights. She let no one think she lacked a mind of her own. The race and sex couldn't afford that, she'd say, when men of her race and class objected to her vigorous leadership. Some clubwomen chose to remain unmarried, some married late in life; some acquired husbands who worked with or for them, then departed after a decade or so. Some made marriage their second profession, in which case they were perfect ladies in the home: mistresses of the social and domestic arts. Of perfect comportment.

Charlotte Hawkins Brown

"If there be anything like a colored lady, I want you to be one": such was the destiny conferred on the young girl through her white great-aunt, her colored grandmother, and her colored mother.

"It was a challenge that burnt its way into my very soul," said Charlotte Hawkins Brown.

Lottie Hawkins was born in North Carolina, in 1883, but the family moved to Cambridge, Massachusetts, when she was five. There they opened a laundry and a boardinghouse that catered to Harvard students. Lottie studied art and music and attended the excellent Cambridge English School. She longed to go to Radcliffe. She also longed to wear a silk slip under her organdie high school graduation gown. The other (white) girls are wearing them, she told her mother. I cannot afford that, Mother replied. Organdie, yes, but if you want the silk slip you must earn the money for it.

So Charlotte Eugenia—she had changed her name, thinking how it would look on her diploma—found a babysitting job. And one day while walking (or sitting) in a Cambridge park, she was observed guiding (or holding) a baby carriage in one hand and a Latin book in the other. The interested observer could see she was reading Virgil in the original and the interested observer was Mrs. Alice Freeman Palmer, former (and first female) president of Wellesley College. Mrs. Palmer asked if she was a student, and if so, where; soon after, Mrs. Palmer visited the school principal to inquire about the precocious colored girl. Then Mrs. Palmer turned her attention elsewhere.

So much for Wellesley or Radcliffe. Charlotte's mother thought it was high time she stopped attending school and started teach-

ing it. Mother and daughter compromised on the two-year State
Normal College in nearby Salem. But the daughter refused to
be deprived of a higher destiny. In Salem, when she discovered
Mrs. Palmer was on the State Board of Education, "I immedi-
ately decided that I would write and tell her that I was the little
brown-skinned girl whom she had seen wheeling the baby carriage and reading Virgil." She asked for a recommendation; Mrs.
Palmer replied with an offer of financial aid.

Five years later Charlotte opened her own two-year school for
Negro children in Sedalia, North Carolina. In 1902 it became
the Palmer Memorial Institute. From the start Charlotte longed
for a liberal arts curriculum. Her white donors, mostly women,
felt that beyond basic literacy, the boys should be taught agricul-
tural and industrial skills and the girls domestic arts like sewing, table setting, and millinery. One Northern donor spoke
for many when she told Brown that "neither their parents, their
possible husbands or they themselves are yet ready to receive"
the benefits of higher education. "Your pupils are not like you,"
another warned. Rural Southern Negroes had not had her exceptional upbringing; they could not be taught "more than
what at present their natures are ready to receive."

She never stopped fund-raising and negotiating; she never
ceased her quest for self-improvement and enhancement. The
Radcliffe dream was replaced with summer courses at Harvard;
there she met and married another teacher in 1911. Edmund
Brown came with her to Palmer and taught; a year later he'd
taken another job, and by 1915 their marriage was done. Proxy
motherhood was just beginning; she helped raise and educate
her relatives' children, seven in all.

And gradually, through the decades, her focus turned away
from white donors and toward the growing Negro middle class;

from industrial and vocational training to the liberal arts, and to Negro parents eager to send their children to a preparatory and finishing school that taught academics and social graces.

"What kind of pictures do we select for our homes, for our children to look upon?" she asked in a 1929 speech. "Are there many Negroes to whom a real symphony would be a treat?"

I can't not roll my eyes here. "Do we care to listen to Bach, Schubert, Beethoven?" she asks. To which I reply: Are you aware, Mrs. Brown, that the economy has just crashed about "our" heads? But Mrs. Brown's work survived the Depression and she kept on, presiding over Palmer's move into the Negro elite, presiding over Negro women's clubs, with their mission of civil rights and improvement for the race at large.

By the Second World War, she had become headmistress, patroness, and doyenne of Negro manners. Nineteen forty-one saw the publication of her etiquette book, *The Correct Thing: To Do—to Say—to Wear.* Amy Vanderbilt wouldn't publish *her* national best seller until 1952. Perfect correctness, perfect manners—perfect fluency in the language of etiquette, perfect mastery of comportment's rituals. It's more than a tool, it's a conquest when you've been told that, like higher education, or high art, it is beyond your capacities.

The "Correct Things," according to Charlotte Hawkins Brown—*Buy mother a box of handkerchiefs and father a tie when you get your allowance. They will appreciate it thoroughly. Eat slowly and noiselessly. Don't "feed." Excessive movements of the body are very ungraceful. Remember that dancing should be done with the feet, not the torso. Do not use the train or public convey-ance for grooming which should be done in private quarters. The inconspicuous use of a powder puff or the smoothing of ruffled hair is all right. A gentleman is never rude. If he can afford ser-*

vants, his real self can be best judged by his attitude to his infe-riors in position—though they render him service of a menial nature—together chart a people's civil progress and spiritual development.

"Dear Friend," she addresses her reader, why another etiquette book when scores exist already? She answers with a missionary passion that drives her to syntactic strain: "Out of the hearts of a humble people has come the desire for recognition of those vital qualities of soul which they feel and cultivate from time to time, but are thwarted in their attempt to express for lack of the knowledge of the best means of expression."

"To Do and to Say and to Wear" means nothing less than To Think and to Feel and to Be. No detail can be overlooked—not "At Home," "At Church," "At The Concert, Theatre or Mov-ies," or "At The Telephone." (No shouting, and be sure to say "Please" and "I thank you" to the operator.) From how the ideal hostess entertains to how the ideal employee behaves at work. From basic cleanliness ("Do not substitute alcohol rubs or toilet water swabbings for cold or tepid showers. Perfume will not take the place of good 'sudsy' water") to savoir faire (" 'Being agree-able' is the highest duty of any human being mingling with other people. . . . Practicing good manners should be as natural as displaying the teeth").

Clearly there are three intense pedagogical drives here: to uplift the masses, to improve the strivers, and to safeguard the behavior of those who've already arrived. And there are implicit or explicit social dramas on almost every page. The sons of laborers are now riding in Pullman cars; they must be taught how to treat the porters and be well treated in return: to ensure they receive good service. "If you go to the dining car, be at home. Display your best taste. The waiters recognize quickly well-bred gentlemen and give them a gentleman's service." In certain states and department stores, Negro women are being allowed to try on hats they wish to buy: "Do not go to buy a hat when your hair has been freshly oiled. The clerk cannot risk having several hats spoiled with grease." Little courtesies make for "a fine and gracious personality," and a fine and gracious personality makes it possible to meet strangers—and the Negro must meet so many white strangers—without "fear or dread."

Ominous words, *fear* and *dread*. Mrs. Brown is trying to give her readers a practice and faith that will shield them from the practical and emotional assaults of bigotry. From the slights and threats of white strangers. And she is telling them, sotto voce, that those bigoted strangers they cannot help meeting are people without grace or fineness—people who, in those essential ways, are their inferiors.

This urgency courses beneath her calm prose demeanor. Poise, she counsels, develops a "calm and undisturbed soul" that can cope with unpleasant situations. Bland and decorous words, but her example of an unpleasant situation is a car accident. The poised individual will notify authorities, find the nearest garage, and supply first aid "without fluttering or excitement." How did poise encounter danger so quickly? In those days car accidents on Southern roads that left Negroes unattended or ill-attended were notorious. Mrs. Brown and her readers surely knew of at least two famous cases: the 1931 crash that led to the death of Juliette Derricotte, Fisk University's dean of women, and the 1937 crash that caused the death of Bessie Smith, Empress of the Blues.

"If there is such a thing as a colored lady, I want you to be one." Lottie Hawkins turned this matriarchal conditional into a triumphant positive. She proved that there are such things as colored ladies and gentlemen, and that, led by her, this precious class would thrive, and enhance the race.

For so many of that Talented Tenth generation, manners, like education, proved that one was equal to all and superior to most. Their power was deeply seductive. Like a chivalric code, Negro manners could be seen as having aesthetic, social, and spiritual dimensions. Erotic ones as well: there is (or can be) something highly seductive about the process of mastering and submitting to them. It's especially exciting if you've been told that you and your people are unfit for such things. Putting people in their place is deeply satisfying when they've always presumed to put you in yours. Oh, to be a lady of color emboldened to discourage strangers who become "too familiar" on a bus or train: "answer them in such a way as to remain polite but have them know that you do not care to be further engaged."

But it all began with the child in thrall to her vision of benevolent white aristocrats. Charlotte Hawkins Brown spent her youth entranced by the ways of cultivated white New Englanders. Her mother, she writes, taught her to be kind, polite, and generous *"in her own way"* (the italics are mine); that chasm acknowledged, she hails the Anglo-Saxon gentry "who in schools and homes teeming with cultural atmosphere gave me an opportunity to observe the fine art of living."

This was her route to freedom. She simply could not see the ethical dangers. The social absurdities. The spiritual confines.

"The arrangement of one's hair adds to or detracts from one's general appearance as it increases or decreases one's power of personality.

"Study the contours of your face carefully. What makes

Katharine Hepburn or Greta Garbo or Marian Anderson *personality plus* may make you *personality minus*": so wrote Charlotte Hawkins Brown in her chapter on good grooming. But in the pictures of Marian Anderson I grow up seeing, there is none of the personality-plus allure girls of my generation crave. There is correctness, there is severe elegance, there is solemnity. We respect and honor Anderson: she is a pioneering artist for our people. And because her art is high Western art, she too must be a Clubwoman. There is nothing provocative or mysterious about her, there is no air of carefree hauteur. In photographs, the folds of Marian Anderson's hair are prohibitively exact. It's as though a doll maker constructed them, then glued them to her strong head to neutralize a face: the face so many would have seen as the stoic one of an African man, with the wide, full lips Caucasians said prevented Negroes from being able to properly perform the classics. We are in the middle of the twentieth century, but the pressed and coiled hair serves her image as the white bonnet served Sojourner Truth's nearly a hundred years before. Once she had left disreputable plantation life behind and begun speaking of equal rights to audiences of Northern whites and Negroes, a more genteel appearance was required.

"Ain't I a woman?" Sojourner thundered at a women's rights convention in 1851, a woman who "could work as much and eat as much as a man—when I could get it—and bear the lash as well." See her then, photographed years after in a diminutive white bonnet enhanced by a freshly laundered white collar and white shawl, whose fringe is echoed by a line of yarn, fist now curled around knitting needles and cane.

Marian Anderson's "Ain't I a Woman" moment came on April 9, 1939. Our parents and grandparents hailed the news and heard the radio broadcast with joy:

MARIAN ANDERSON, REFUSED A CONCERT HALL BY THE
DAUGHTERS OF THE AMERICAN REVOLUTION, SINGS OUT-
SIDE AT THE LINCOLN MEMORIAL.

At the Lincoln Memorial

The finished statue of Abraham Lincoln is nineteen feet tall and
carved from twenty-eight blocks of white Georgia marble. The
French had special lighting installed to enhance the figure of the
man born in a Kentucky log cabin.

The finished person of Marian Anderson is five feet ten
inches of brown flesh mounted on white bone, originating in a
modest section of Philadelphia and smoothed and polished in
the capitals of Europe.

The president who saved the Union wears a suit, vest, and
bow tie. The woman who reaffirms the Union's highest purpose
wears a black mink coat, a hat, and a jeweled scarf of orange and
yellow (key tones in the Negro skin palette).

He sits, legs foursquare and apart, as if he could shelter the
whole world between them. The premier contralto of her people
stands waiting for her cue to become immortal.

Above his head are carved the words:

IN THIS TEMPLE AS IN THE HEARTS OF THE PEOPLE FOR
WHOM HE SAVED THE UNION THE MEMORY OF ABRAHAM
LINCOLN IS ENSHRINED FOREVER.

The piano sounds the introduction. She fingers her necklace
and arranges her head to look upon the throngs.

From the lips of "a daughter of the race from which he struck
the chains of slavery" come the words "My country, 'tis of thee,
Sweet land of liberty . . ." and—right then—enshrined for-

ever in our memories is the change she makes. *"Of thee I sing"* becomes "To *thee* We *sing."* The singular pronoun of a sheltered citizen becomes the plural pronoun of an embattled people who must address (speak to), not possess (speak of), their country.

She wasn't allowed a singular identity except when she sang: there you could hear her stroking, savoring tones and syllables, in a private ecstasy.

So much melancholy, I think, reading these pages. But why choose that word instead of "depression"? "Depression" has gone flat from so much use. I mistrust "depression" because it's too easy (for me, anyway) to forget the rage, even petulance, inside it. "Melancholy" is prettier than "depression"; it connotes a kind of nocturnal grace. Makes one feel more innocently beleaguered.

In point of fact, those of us who avoided disaster encountered life's usual rewards and pleasures, obstacles and limitations. If we still had some longing for death, we had to make it compatible with this new pattern of living.

All that circumnavigating of race, class, and gender made for comedy too. Comic chagrin, comic relief, comic reversals (at least adjustment) of fortune. Sometimes we felt like postmodern topsy-turvy dolls.

So call these a set of relativity tales.

The Seventies

i

It's enter-the-elevator-and-get-to-your-desk-by-10-a.m. rush hour at *Newsweek*. I place myself amid my white colleagues. We're all preoccupied—so much to read, write, convert into like-minded prose. We murmur greetings, trade short sentences, sip at our coffee. The elevator door closes; the elevator starts its climb; we fall silent.

There is one other black in the elevator; a messenger, looking about eighteen or nineteen, there to deliver useful documents to some writer, researcher, or editor's secretary. As the elevator hits 5, his voice sounds out, sibilant, insistent, insidious.

"*Sis*-ter . . ."

If anyone was about to talk, they're not talking now. Into the deepening silence, he flings "Sister BLACK!"

Five floors later, the door finally opens.

I exit, trying not to rush.

Look back at him with narrowed eyes, register the assiduously blank faces of the remaining whites.

Watch the door close on his gleeful smirk.

ii

Peachie is talking to her Italian boyfriend. "In our world, when I grew up it was an advantage to have straight hair," she tells him. "But even then it made me self-conscious."

His brow is genuinely furrowed when he answers.

"Your hair's not straight," he says.

iii

Our friend Shawn has taken to wearing a voluminous Afro wig on social occasions, especially in the black community. Many politically conscious black women with light skin and straight hair do the same: it's the only way to make sure people acknowledge their racial identity.

On this hot and steamy night at a crowded New Orleans club, the six inches of human hair attached to the synthetic fibers of the wig cap gather so much heat and sweat that Shawn excuses herself and goes to the ladies' room. She is too uncomfortable to notice the other woman there. She bends over the sink, closes her eyes, pulls off the wig, and shakes it hard, trying to dislodge the sweat drops. When she straightens up, she sees the woman removing a wig too, shaking it, trying to dislodge the sweat drops, taking a comb from her purse to run through the wig's long, straight locks, coaxing its limp ends back into their flip curve, and taking a paper towel to the bangs.

The mirror invites their eyes to meet. Shawn takes in the short, crisp frizz on her neighbor's head; the neighbor takes in the dead straight, now crumpled shoulder-length hair of Shawn. Then, slowly, in near unison, they put their wigs back on and leave the bathroom in silence.

The Eighties

i

Peachie, Joan, and I are at a book party. Writers and other artists chat and cluster with friends, lovers, and prospects. We three start a race talk, not a serious one, just a lighthearted trading of insider tales. I've found that at white gatherings—parties, concerts—blacks often talk like this for a few minutes. As if to say *We know your world and we know ours too. How many of you could say the same?*

And this is especially pleasing tonight, since two of us aren't obviously black. (And they keep a working list of white people's race ID gaffes *Are you Mediterranean? You look Sephardic. Is one of your parents black? Mixed race?*) Peachie jokes that sometimes, to head off the wrong kind of remark—you never know what a white person will say about blacks to White People Only—she begins every available sentence with "As a black woman . . . ," for instance, "As a black woman who's ordering a cappuccino . . ."

Why are we three talking about this here and now? Do we, as the only blacks present, feel the need to condescend, gain an edge over this roomful of chattering whites?

"But 'talking black' is too simple," says P. "I used to date a white man from Mississippi and I'd always find myself imitating his accent whenever we were together. Which made me sound more 'black' than I ever had."

We laugh. And as we do, a young white man joins us. None of us knows him. He's attractive in a quiet way and his manner isn't intrusive. But his presence is.

How to make this clear without being unpleasant? We smile as if he's welcome. Then P. says: "We were just talking about how seductive black and white Southern accents are. I was saying that when I used to date a white man from Mississippi I'd always end up imitating *his* accent."

He smiles. "I know. I used to date a white man from Mississippi too, and *I'd* always find myself imitating his accent." The emphasis on "I" lets us know he's white. And he's managed a small stylish coup that gives us all pleasure.

"Congratulations," I say. "You've just made yourself the most exotic person in our group."

ii

George and I have been friends since the early seventies. He's gay, and handsome in a manly Western Protestant way, the Gary Cooper way, with a head of healthy chestnut hair that falls lightly over his left brow; craggy yet refined features; a lean body fit for tailored khakis and button-down shirts or tight blue Levis with black bomber jackets. He was my first close gay friend and I was his first close black friend.

Which has led to confusions we cherish.

When we go to largely heterosexual parties together, white women drawn to him give me appraising or irritated looks, then move in.

When we pass gay white men on the street, they cut me and give him smoldering glances.

When we pass gay black men on the street, they shoot me a *Girlfriend, you should know better* look, then turn to him with a sly smile or a playful moue.

And when we pass heterosexual black men on the street, they narrow their eyes at me and mutter or sneer, "What do you need that white man for, sister?"

The Nineties

i

The place is Chez Josephine, the New York restaurant consecrated to the first international female superstar of the Negro race. Her image is on every wall, her creamy brown flesh, oiled, stretched, stroked into feathers, beads, sequins, banana belts; the saucy grin, the dimpled cheeks and knees seducing, mocking, exalting, enticing visitors of every age and hue.

The time is late January 1993.

Two black women in their mid-forties sit talking about the two famous people who have died that week and been ceaselessly commemorated. One of the women, she of the voluminous Afro wig, is still pale beige, her naturally straight hair now on view. The other is me, a light-but-definite-brown, with naturally frizzy hair.

Shawn leans forward, moves her wineglass out of the way. Lowering her voice, she looks around to make sure the people at nearby tables can hear nothing. Then she speaks.

Softly:

"You know, in a way, Audrey Hepburn's death meant more to me than Thurgood Marshall's."

"I know," I answer, leaning in and quickly looking around again. The neighbors are definitely not listening. (And if the restaurant pianist could provide a sound track at this moment, it would be the histrionic opening notes of *Now It Can Be Told*.)

Thurgood Marshall secured our right before the Supreme Court of the United States to attend well-funded white public schools. Thurgood Marshall embodied what our parents had overcome to succeed; he had the social conscience all Negroes who succeed should have. He represented valor and constant struggle.

Audrey Hepburn gave us the privilege of a fantasy life, grounded in centuries of cherished European girlhood.

The aristocrat loved by all who see her: Audrey Hepburn, in *Roman Holiday*. The fair daughter of humble people, loyal to her family, gentle yet proud when scorned by the ignorant and haughty, winning the love of the rich and handsome: Audrey Hepburn in *Sabrina*.

Oh, the vehement inner lives of girls snatching at heroines and role models! A maiden emboldened by visions of a destiny beyond herself, willing to suffer martyrdom even as she fights for the poor and helpless: Audrey Hepburn in *The Nun's Story*.

And the longing to suffer nothing at all, to be rewarded, decorated, festooned for one's charm and looks, one's piquant daring, one's winning idiosyncrasies: Audrey Hepburn in *Funny Face* and *Breakfast at Tiffany's*. Equality in America for a bourgeois black girl meant equal opportunity to be playful and winsome. Indulged.

Shawn says: *Those Audrey Hepburn and Doris Day movies summed up all your tiny little fantasies about having a career and a glamorous life in New York or Europe.*

And no—Doris Day is not to be expunged from this record of girlhood fancies, though it's far more embarrassing to admit one's fondness for her foursquare Ohio pluck. (It so helped that Hepburn was European.) Nevertheless, some of us were not too good for Doris Day. Like her, we were midwesterners, schooled, like her, in the ways of perkiness. We brought smiles to dutiful tasks. Our yearning was sprightly.

And Doris Day's singing made Berry Gordy cry. When he was young and still obscure, he wrote a song for her and mailed it (boyishly, reverently) to "Doris Day, Hollywood." He told this story even after he had founded Motown Records and made Diana Ross his muse. He wasn't ashamed. Why should we be? Listen to the lyrics of Martha and the Vandellas' first hit, "Come and Get These Memories." Friendship rings, love letters, teddy bears and state fairs. Turn it into a waltz.

Now it's a Doris Day song.

ii

Denise kisses her white boyfriend goodnight and steps into the waiting taxi. With his long stringy hair and mustache, the driver looks like a Doobie Brother. He's quiet for a few minutes. Then he turns around at a stoplight and smiles. "I saw you and your boyfriend. My girlfriend is black. She says it's hard for her sometimes. Is it hard for you?" Denise of the burnt sienna skin arranges her face to look haughty. "I wouldn't know," she tells him. "Both my parents are white."

Here and Now

I'm reading through 1950s issues of *Ebony,* paying close attention to the hair and skin cream ads. I have a flashback to season three of *Mad Men,* to the episodes where Pete Campbell, snarky scion of a fine old dysfunctional New York family, the Dartmouth man who's always known he's too little and boyish to impress people unless he can shrewdly divert their punitive impulses elsewhere, the aspiring writer chagrined that a colleague of lower-middle-class origin was gifted enough to publish a story in *Harper's*—where that Pete Campbell grows acutely interested in the Negro Market and is seen avidly reading *Ebony* in the privacy of his Madison Avenue office.

A moment I can enjoy with a manageable frisson of horror because I never had to witness it in my youth. It's a primal sociocultural scene, watching a white person discover our secrets for his ends.

Why did I never notice the *Ebony* ads for Kongolene Hair Cream when I was growing up? They're inescapable, irrefutable.

Kongolene Hair Cream for Men:
Logo KKK: (KONGO KONGOLENE KHEMICAL)

First advertised in 1914, as men of color demanded the rights to fight abroad for their country, improve their economic and social lot at home, and wear sumptuously gleaming straight hair brushed back with a middle or side part like Rudy Valentino and Douglas Fairbanks. This demand increased with each decade. The colored Chicago businessman J. D. Murray first advertised his brand of Kongolene in 1925—"You get a waterproof job and your hair stays straight for 20 days. Or more." (Was that the product George Raft was said to go to Harlem for?) Men acquired ridges and waves that sat up proudly (James Cagney in command) or flung themselves about the head and ears wildly (James Cagney under siege); hair that could divide itself into fine long strands and whip from side to side (Robert Mitchum under duress); hair that could rise calmly into a bed of shiny curls and waves (Dean Martin) or into a domed pompadour with nary a wave in sight (James Dean and Elvis Presley).

What did the KKK initials, so dreaded in another context, signify? The three stages:

K1, the pre-crème, protectively saturating hair and scalp, preparing it for

K2, the straightening crème, which assaulted the indigenous kinks with potassium or sodium chloride, followed by

K3, the black rinse, which erased the residue of crinkly, faded, discolored hair.

Surely most Negroes seeing the ad in newspapers could not avoid thinking of the Ku Klux Klan? They had to notice the logo letters, tall and stalwart as the white-sheet warriors in *Birth of a Nation*. Seen how they were sliced through the middle by the banner triumphantly reading "Kongolene." Does the Kongo meet the KKK and transform it, through the Negro man's appropriation of the white man's hair? There's even a gesture toward race pride: "If your druggist cannot supply you," the bottom of the ad counsels, "order direct from KONGO CHEMICAL CO., INC." (New World address: 124th Street, Harlem, U.S.A.)

The battle had gone on for years. Negroes had fought for white hair in their homes, mixing eggs, potatoes, and toxic, burning lye, applying the potion to every hair follicle, enduring the anguish of hot, singed, even burning scalps, the risk of hair disintegrating under the pressure.

The manly KKK discourse had none of the anxious beauty coaching and coaxing found in hair ads for women. With Perma-Strate, "Hair is softly straight without that artificial 'poker-straight' look . . . And one creamy applications lasts 3 to 6 months!" There's little of the longing for desirability and respectability that pervades feminine hair ads. "Even with her hat on . . . you'd know she uses **Vapoil**. Because she's well groomed and smart . . ." (A sore point, this grooming detail— hair oil regularly stains our hat rims and headbands.) "Is your hair inviting to touch?" queries Dixie Peach. (A hit, a palpa- ble hit.) "Yesterday," Silky Strate proclaims, "fire engines were pulled by horses and hair was straightened with hot combs. TODAY . . . you can have naturally-soft, permanently-straight hair the easy MODERN WAY." Longer-looking hair? "No discoloration—no oils—no damage," pledges Lustrasilk. And it's wonderful for your children too.

Then there's the blatant abjection of the skin ads, always directed at women, always promising lighter skin and a brighter life—"Make light of dark skin woes"—within days.

Black and White Bleaching Cream: "Beauty *Is* Skin Deep. Begin now to have lighter, smoother, softer skin that attracts admirers."

Nadinola Bleaching Cream: "Have you noticed that the nicest things happen to girls with lighter, lovelier complexions?" And, as a melancholy woman in a strapless evening dress sits alone, holding a flower and sadly murmuring "He loves me . . . he loves me not . . . DON'T DEPEND ON DAISIES! BE *SURE* WITH A LIGHT, CLEAR COMPLEXION!"

The Miracle Bleach for Dark Skin invented and developed by Golden Peacock is called "The favorite of Dark Skinned TV Stars." (There are such things.) And while Dr. Fred Palmer attempts to modulate his message by claiming his formula gets rid of pimples and blemishes (a common gambit), he bluntly names it what he knows his consumers want it to be: a Double Strength Skin Whitener. You will never be the fair sex, but you strive to be an ever-fairer one.

i

I'm at Ricky's in the West Village, buying the products that keep my hair in its state of artificially enhanced naturalness.

"Hello, how are you today?" The young black man at the counter greets me with well-enunciated courtesy and totals my purchases. "That'll be $84.90," he says, and though his face doesn't react to my furrowed brow, he does add, picking up my credit card and nodding toward the fifty-dollar Devachan Conditioner: "That will last you a long time. It's just a shock right now. Your hair looks very good. These products are good."

"Thank you. It does last," I say. I've regained my assurance. "I have my hair cut and colored at their salon."

"Real-ly?" he says, drawing out the word and moving from clerk comfort-chat to genuine curiosity. "I didn't know they understood our . . ." He needn't say it. HAIR is the word. It leaps into the air between us, binding us through centuries of struggle.

"Their curly hair regimen was invented by an English-woman," I say. "But they've adapted their methods to our hair. They do all kinds of curly hair. There are always other black women there. Black and Latina stylists too."

Does he need quite this much information? He still looks politely inquiring, so I go on. I feel I must articulate what we both know to be the chasm that divides "curly hair" as seen by white women vs. black women. And one reason I love going to my salon is that, unlike so many white salons I've taken my head to (sometimes finding the one black stylist, sometimes choosing the white one recommended by an informed friend), I feel I bring Old World authority to this New World Order. Who more than I embodies the new ascendancy of Naturally Curly Hair?

"Ummmmmm," he registers. "Do you mind if I ask you a question?"

"Of course not," I say brightly.

"What is your ethnic ancestry?"

Proceed with care, Margo. You're taken aback.

"I'm African American," I tell him. I usually say "black," since it was my generation's breakthrough word, and "African American" feels textbook-officious in everyday talk. So why do I use it now? Because he wants an answer that conveys precision. Because I want to provide precision since his skin is black-brown and mine is cream-brown; since he is dressed in monochromatic black that sets off the black-brown gleam of his face and shaved head; since his diction and manner make clear he is a young gay black/African-American man-about-town who lives by making distinctions.

So I say, "I'm African American."

And he says, "*Real*-ly?" slightly widening his eyes, tilting his head, and tucking his chin a little bit out and forward.

"Well," I hedge, reaching for the "We" that will bracket and bind us together once more, "you know, we all—so many of us—if you go back far enough—we've all got some white, some Indian ancestry, we're such a mix . . ." Yes, he's nodding, concurring, and I'm stumbling a bit because I'm anxious he might declare (proudly? sternly? mischievously?), "Not me. I have no white or Indian ancestors." But he doesn't. He nods, murmurs "Um-hmmm," and widens his eyes again, saying, "A lot of people must ask you that."

I don't want to correct him; that might make him feel I think it's a naïve question.

"I wouldn't say a lot, but at intervals people do ask, it's true," I concede. Then go on to offer: "You know, when people ask I think it's because there are lots of Latinos who have my general looks, and"—here I give a comic one-beat pause—"I think it's because I color my hair blonde. If I were still a brunette not so many people would ask."

I get the laugh I sought and consider further ingratiating myself by adding, "Of course my natural color is gray now." No. That cedes too much authority.

I move back to Our Hair turf.

"Devachan understands the mechanics of hair that goes from curly to frizzy to"—and here comes my coup de theatre— "nappy." Ah, *nappy*. The word seals our bond. He laughs, covering his mouth with one hand.

"It's been a while since you thought about *that* word," I say, and we give the exultant sotto voce chortle of Negroes sharing a naughty fact of race life in public.

ii

When I was told by a friendly acquaintance (white) that he and another acquaintance (white) had been told by a former friend of

mine (black), "Oh, Margo thinks she's a white woman," I grew
irate. There'd been tensions between us. But to humiliate me
like that, so deliberately, so gleefully! If he'd said it to friendly
black acquaintances, I'd have been irate but not mortified—
seen it as a personal attack using predictably handy race rhetoric
as a shorthand for other resentments. (He wasn't wrong to feel
I'd been neglecting him lately, returning his calls but not initiat-
ing my own.) There was the risk that these black acquaintances
would agree, which I would resent. But I felt I could rebut the
charge in my own mind. Over the years I'd built up resistance
to those toxins. The situation that pertained here was trickier. I
faced the likelihood of the white audience being nonplussed and
intimidated. They might reason (without telling me, naturally),
"Well, being black, he can see her racially in a way we can't.
Maybe she really does have an identity problem." Or "This is all
very sad. We don't know exactly what he means, but we're not
going to pursue it because clearly this is racial damage territory
and, for all their accomplishments, it shows the racial damage
they've both suffered."

I despised that kind of pity.

A few months later a white friend was telling me how a nasty
remark had made its slow, lethal way to her. "Has anyone ever
told you something someone else said about you, something
mean, but not, if you looked at it squarely, completely untrue?"
asked Laurie.

"Why, yes," I said and told my tale. She started to laugh.
"That's all?" she said.

"Please remember the combustible psychological and political and sociological history of this charge," I chastised.

"You're right," she answered. "I don't mean to trivialize it. I
know it has a fraught history, and you know the details much
better than I."

"I do indeed," I asserted. "A fraught history with many roots. Start with self-hatred and arrogance if you really *are* trying to be white; start with envy and ignorance if you're falsely accusing someone of trying to be. Actually, I think he was attacking what he saw as a certain snobbishness in me, a way of distancing myself, and a tendency to cherish my neuroses as a sign of my specialness."

"Is that really worse," she asked, "than being called a predatory narcissist?"

"Why, no," I said. "Actually it's not."

And went my way rejoicing.

Once, maybe ten years ago, I told a lover, "Actually, I'm as white as I am black." He'd picked up something of mine—a CD, a book—and said, teasingly, "Not a lot of black folk like Elly Ameling." My retort still felt dangerous to say out loud, despite all the talk of hybridity, creolization, cosmopolitanism, and mulatto consciousness. "Sometimes I almost forget I'm a Negro," my mother wrote seventy years ago. It wasn't a disavowal; it was her claim to a free space. She was talking about her happiness at that moment— how you feel when everything inside and around you is where it belongs. How you feel when your rights in America are self-evident, not to be argued, justified, or brooded on every day. Those seventy years had won me the right to claim any part of any culture without any race-linked restriction. "Claim"? Consider. Study. Toy with. And when I choose, love.

From the earliest rocking of my cradle I went A. A. Milne–ing and Kenneth Grahame–ing along, amid the Negroisms of family, friends, and neighbors. My father's sepulchral "When-whenwhenwhen," as he imitated the sermon of a Mississippi preacher. How a man would raise his arm, slap the air, bring the arm down in an arc, and start to turn away, meaning "Man, don't try that on me." Grown-up voices running through the tones and syntax of white and black speech. My mother's "The discussion is closed," all quick-pace martial consonants, then her "I'm not studying you" (which I heard as "stutting"), high in the throat, pitch descending on "m" and "not," downbeat on "stutt."

How many pieces of journalism have I written where my race might as well have been invisible? Then I'd choose a subject that made it the guiding principle. Or an approach that refused to let a subject be solely white or black.

There's not only Du Bois's warring double consciousness. Or the dual personality James Weldon Johnson described, where we perform in the generic style each race demands. There's a space in our consciousness where all this racialized material collects, never static, mutating or at least recombining.

How many times could we write our cultural life stories? How many selves would tell them?

A Retelling: *Little Women*

In 1994, with the third movie version en route to theaters and two new editions of the novel in bookstores, I decide to reread *Little Women,* putting up with looks I get from teenage girls on the bus or subway who must think I'm emotionally regressed or a very slow reader.

And it all becomes clear to me: I should have wanted to be Amy.

Meg is so pretty, so temptingly pretty, and with her native sweetness, her gentle ways—well, that's why Meg is out of the question. Here you are, smoothly uttering Victorian commonplaces you thought you'd cleansed your stock of forty years ago. Meg does have her vanities, the kind pretty girls are entitled to, the kind plain and pretty readers avidly share—" 'It's so dreadful to be poor!' sighed Meg, looking down at her old dress."

These are all that keep her from insurmountable dullness, even as she guides her young sisters toward the dull ideal of good womanly manners.

"You are old enough to leave off boyish tricks and to behave better, Josephine . . . you should remember that you are a young lady."

"As for you, Amy, you are altogether too particular and prim. Your airs are funny now, but you'll grow up an affected little goose if you don't take care."

Decorum will protect Meg from the twists of fate and plot that impose suffering. She will marry a man as good-looking and good-hearted as she. (Wiser and more good-hearted, that he may teach and guide her.) They will have twins, a boyish boy and a girlish girl. Here is the little New England cottage where they will settle. Imagine a BLESS OUR HOME mat woven by Meg's own hands in front of the door. Then let the door close. There's no need to give Meg any more serious thought.

Hail Jo, wielding the pen of the artist and the sword of the girl who knows she should have been a boy. What girl didn't want to be Jo at least some of the time, Jo of the restless impulses, the unruly luxuriant hair; shouting, grumbling, flinging retorts instead of answers; thrusting her body into unruly poses. The swashbuckling hero bent on astonishing everyone and being a rich and famous writer.

Jo gives license to outbursts. Her sulks are theatrically compelling and her indignation is always warranted. Jo's at the center of every page she strides or saunters onto. She has charisma and that's what you've always craved.

A functional definition of charisma for ambitious girls of the

1950s: winning the attention, touched with wonder, of significant adults (teachers, relatives, family friends); winning the friendship of gifted, temperamentally interesting, or socially accomplished girls; winning admiration from boys or, under circumstances that don't turn them against you, winning contests with boys.

Being "gifted" in a way that can't go unnoticed. We seek models everywhere—in books and movies, in serious TV dramas and frolicsome sitcoms; in prima ballerinas and leading ladies; in star turns on TV variety shows. ("Ladies and gentlemen, here is the enchanting . . . Ladies and gentlemen, here is the dynamic . . . Ladies and gentlemen, please welcome a young woman who's been making quite a stir on Broadway these days. . . .")

Can you be a waif and a powerhouse like Judy Garland? An incandescent eccentric like Tammy Grimes? I've learned already that adults are won over by remarks they find precocious but not sassy. I'm very good at that. I've learned that personality gets you roles in school plays and report card comments on your ability to lead.

Where will this take me? All my teachers say I write well. I've published a poem in a magazine for young Negro readers, edited by Charlaemae Rollins, the pioneering children's librarian at Bronzeville's distinguished and first public library. Still, I don't scribble away in a happy daze like Jo or play my piano with Beth's rapture. I'm quick with my words and my wit, but I don't distinguish myself by winningly unconventional behavior.

Jo wants to be a rich and famous writer. Does she want to marry? She tosses her head and says no, again no. But marry she must, for Louisa May Alcott, thirty-seven and still unmarried, must tend to the needs of her readers, those marriage-minded young girls who will make her famous and nearly rich, those "dear girls," she calls them placatingly, who scorn old maids.

The Jo who proclaimed she'd astonish everyone at twenty-two is mightily humbled on the eve of her twenty-fifth birthday.

"An old maid—that's what I'm to be," she muses, laying her body down on an old worn sofa at twilight. "A literary spinster, with a pen for a spouse, a family of stories for children, and twenty years hence a morsel of fame, perhaps; when, like Johnson I'm too old, and can't enjoy it—solitary, and can't share it, independent, and don't need it."

Here Alcott steps anxiously in. Girls like Jo may despair, she counsels; not all blossoming girls will blossom into wives and mothers. Yet and still, "one can get on quite happily if one has something in one's self to fall back upon."

That bleak, immolating phrase: "something . . . to fall back upon"! Alcott means character, often neglected or underdeveloped in girls; by our day it means a college or graduate degree that will let us teach, or get a just-as-respectable job, if we're edged off the two-parent-family path by death, divorce, or spinsterhood.

Of course my peers and I will all have college or graduate degrees to fall back on.

Was our character in the Alcott sense neglected? When I was overheard gleefully reporting one friend's secret to another ("I'm not supposed to tell anybody, but . . ."), my mother sat me down for a talk on being trustworthy. "You have personality, but personality isn't enough," she told me. "You have to have character too."

I will have something in myself to fall back on.

I wear thick glasses and I am thrilled by narratives of beautiful women attracting handsome men: sweetly vulnerable maidens needing rescue; heroines who are daring and must be won by still more daring men. Brought down to its basic learning level: fate finds a way to award desirable boys to pretty girls. I worry that I won't attract boys as pretty girls do, that I'll be excluded from all

*these burning glances and kisses, these scenes of enraptured pursuit,
followed by a match that makes the family rejoice and the world
approve. I have no taste for being excluded from any of this.*

"Don't laugh at the spinsters, . . . for often very tender, tragi-
cal romances are hidden away in the hearts that beat so quietly
under the sober gowns," Alcott pleads. "Even the sad, sour sisters," the kind on Old Maid cards, deserve our pity, "because
they have missed the sweetest part of life."

I have no taste for being passed over and pitied.

Alcott has no taste for being pitied, passed over, or married. She
wants Jo to be like her, a literary spinster.

No! say her readers; please no! says her publisher. So she
works out the assets and deficits of the marriage, as women in
life must. She won't indulge those who want Jo to marry Laurie,
still handsome and charming, still willful and idly rich. Is she
denying Jo what she denied herself—a lovably erotic companion? Is she negotiating more emotional power and independence
for her? The March girls have struggled too long with deprivation; it's only fair that Laurie suffer as well—be humbled by his
love for unwomanly Jo, then by her refusal to love him back. If
she loved him, she'd have to feel grateful he chose her. And he
would surely hold the power of his looks, his money, his status,
over her. Despite his best intentions, he wouldn't be able to help
himself. That's how the world worked.

*These kinds of considerations arose whenever the subject of mixed
marriage was discussed. A white husband would always be aware of
how his family, friends, and associates saw you, of what marrying
you cost him in the world. And you'd always be trying to make it
up to him.*

He couldn't help turning on you at some point.

Readers will get the appropriate match when Amy and Laurie marry. For Jo they must accept the consolations of philosophy in the form of a stout middle-aged professor with big hands, rusty clothes, and without "a handsome feature in his face except his beautiful teeth." He teaches her German, he gives her a volume of Shakespeare, he defends Christianity against agnosticism. When he divines that Jo is publishing "sensational" stories under a pseudonym, his response (grievous sorrow rather than anger) has a New Testament power.

No more lurid adventures, no more illicit passions erupting in foreign/exotic locales. Jo retreats to her room, reads her stories, and stuffs them in the stove, "nearly setting the chimney afire with the blaze." Then, like one of her merry wrongdoers, she adds, "I almost wish I hadn't any conscience, it's so inconvenient . . . I can't help wishing, sometimes, that father and mother hadn't been so dreadfully particular about such things."

But, ah Jo, Alcott intervenes, in the voice that drove Baldwin to immolate her without mercy: "pity from your heart those who have no such guardians to hedge them round with principles which may seem like prison walls to impatient youth, but which will prove sure foundations to build character upon in womanhood."

There's no help for it. Jo must marry Professor Bhaer. The End again—and one the most morally dutiful girl reader struggles with. You don't want to be a pitiful spinster, but must your only choice be a kind and dowdy man who already has two children—orphan nephews—you must start caring for right away?

And not them alone. By the novel's end, Jo has been dis-

persed into the bodies and souls of boy after boy: the boys she
gives birth to; the boys she brings into her all-boys school; an
endless, boundless "wilderness of boys."

It was not for me.

But those discontents belonged to the second volume of *Little
Women,* not to the all-consuming Book One. Meg, Jo, Beth,
Amy: there, in the character and personality of a March girl,
you could place a second beguiling self.

Denise had tomboy leanings, and she could stage fiery displays of will. She claimed Jo as soon as we read the book in
grade school, and being three years older, she managed to read
it first, striding through the house reciting Jo's lines and enacting Alcott's directions: "Christmas won't be Christmas without
any presents," she'd grumble, then fling herself down on our
living room rug. "We don't cheat in America; but *you* can, if you
choose," she'd angrily tell Ned, the British twit I was imperson-
ating, then stride past me, and exit.

I was not going to be left with Meg. I had no desire to take
on, even in imagination, the caretaking duties of an elder sister.
And I had a near-compulsive sense of social order. No, that's
evasive. I had a near-compulsive sense of how biology orders
social expectations, and how I should respond. In third grade,
taking some kind of school test with the question "Which parent do you love most?," I (falsely) put my father's name first,
then—compulsively—explained to my mother that I'd done
this because fathers were the heads of families, so should be seen
as the most loved. "If that's what you wrote, that's what they'll
believe," she said, a little bleakly.

So even if Meg had tempted me, I couldn't have made myself
violate the birth order of our family. Now, hoping to ease the
shame of my conformity, I posit that I was resisting an alter ego

who would exacerbate it. An appealing fancy, which evaporates
when you consider that

I

chose

Beth.

The sweetest of daughters, the dearest of sisters. "Little Tranquility," her father calls her. "Birds in their little nests agree,"
she sings when her sisters quarrel, and their quarrels cease. She
is loved by all who know her, and she need not struggle to win
love; she makes no effort to win love: she is loved because she is
loving. Being good brings her pleasure. Nature and nurture are
one here. Beth's only failing is her shyness. It's acute enough to
seem, at times, a form of selfishness. But she struggles with it; she
is one of those good people ever ready to find fault with herself.
(I didn't want the burden of painful shyness, but my vivacity
sometimes got me into trouble.) Beth loves music. She plays the
piano (as did I), and her music brings joy to lonely neighbors.
Hers is a quiet, modest gift. (Mine, I hoped, was more vivid and
striking.) Still, it gives her some parity with writer Jo and artist
Amy. And Beth's music gives her some release from the expressive confines of goodness; different tempos and dynamics are
briefly possible.

Until fatal illness does away with her when she is just eighteen. I must have found it seductive even as a girl: death as the
villain who destroys you; death as the savior who ensures your
spotless reputation. Is it possible, as an adult, to read the death
of Beth without dissolving into self-protective mockery? Actually, yes, with a certain amount of readerly discipline. At last a
few human flaws appear. Envy: "But when I saw you all so well,
and strong, and full of happy plans, it was hard to feel that I
never could be like you." Despair: "She could not say 'I'm glad

to go,' for life was very sweet to her; she could sob out 'I'll try to be willing . . .'" and give in to bitter grief. Dying was a way of giving in to every emotion and remaining beyond criticism.

But what are we to do about Amy? Meg's soft prettiness takes on the chill of the snow maiden in Amy; Meg's vanity turns voracious. Jo's will becomes willfulness; her pride veers into egotism. Not for a moment can Amy be selflessly generous. When she is good, she must boast of being good; when she is sorry for being thoughtless—or greedy or snobbish—she must frame her apology with self-congratulation or self-justification. Amy has a talent: she draws and paints. But not with Beth's quiet devotion, not with Jo's gusto. When Amy paints, she pulls our attention to her: we are to admire how attractive she looks doing it.

Older sisters have basked alone in the attention of parents; grappled alone with the power of parents; they hoard precious memories of child-rule; they never forget the moment they were to give space and attention to the new child. (The night I was born my sister drank a bottle of mineral oil.) They have little patience with someone who does all the things they've had to grow out of. Yet they're expected to instruct and help the young intruder, to be little parents.

They demand our obedience; they enjoy our admiration.

We crave their approval. We study them, learn their ways. And we hate being shown up by them, making mistakes that are shamefully obvious because the older sibling made them first or claims she was too smart to make them at all. We fight for power with the tricks of the weak—tattling, wheedling, acts of sabotage. And we need them in a way they don't need us. This can feel like your first experience of unrequited love.

When I was growing up, no girl I knew would admit she wanted to be Amy. Alcott made sure you would not choose Amy unless you were willing to be mocked or reproved on almost every page. The word "little" zaps her again and again—her little airs and graces, her little clay figurines, her little sister tricks and errors. Only her pretensions are grand: an English stuffed with malapropisms; atrocious spelling and "punchtuation"; reading French aloud to her little friends "without mispronouncing more than two-thirds of the words." When Amy's not allowed to tag along to the theater with Jo, Meg, and Laurie, her revenge is stunning. She turns into a twelve-year-old Hedda Gabler and burns Jo's writings.

But because these little women are pilgrims, and because Alcott is prey to the environmental effects of Christian sentimentality, Amy's character improves once she is chastened. By the time she wins Laurie's love and money, she knows that he loved Jo first, and that she must renounce her art because her talent is hopelessly minor.

I had a talent for which I had won praise. My personality, not my looks, won attention. I hated being mocked by my older sister when I made gaffes. I liked to think of myself as a good person. I wanted to be loved unequivocally. I wanted to deserve that love without question. I wanted to be in a position where I was never reproved or corrected by my mother, where I never lost a quarrel—or had to quarrel and risk losing—with my sister, where I felt she adored me every minute of the day, and where I never had to struggle to win the approval of friends and schoolmates. It would be so restful to want no more than you had and to be perfect, in life and in people's memories.

At least Amy had appetite. Insistence. She would have given me more aptitude, more tolerance for risk—for willfulness—for wanting and saying I did, even when I made a fool of myself and didn't get it.

Taking a race line, I could argue that on an Anglo-Saxon dreamscape it was better to choose a brunette than a blue-eyed blonde. But I'd already bonded with dark-haired Margaret

O'Brien and feisty, ugly Mary Lennox. I was tainted but relatively intact. It was my temperament that had threatened to do me in.

A Retelling: The Clubwomen

The grandmothers were enthralling. Improvising dowager status for themselves. Mine had both grown up in Mississippi, gone to Rust College, and taught in small country schools. They both worked in dressmaking when they moved North (the Jeffersons to Denver, then Los Angeles; the McClendons to St. Louis and, for my grandmother, Chicago). They planned their children's educational ascent with vigilance. They plotted their own advancement with equal care.

Women of color born between 1880 and 1905 seized hold of Progress and faced down Peril on all fronts. Encouraged by the example of their own formidable parents, they became teachers and dressmakers and caterers, nurses and stenographers, even doctors and lawyers. They opened beauty shops and Sunday schools. They learned to keep accounts for the men who founded insurance companies and funeral homes. They sometimes married these men; they often outlived them and took over the business. But if they'd married men who had little to leave, they set out to earn doweries for their daughters. They passed for white to sell clothes in white department stores. They took in boarders. They studied property values and bought real estate. (Every week, tenants placed their rent in the courteous, peremptory hand of the dowager.)

My maternal grandmother, Lily McClendon Armstrong, had a two-year-old daughter when she lost her husband to the flu epidemic of 1918. He'd been an engineer, hired by Booker T. Washington and sent by him to Purdue for graduate training. When he died, Lily and baby Irma moved from Holly Springs, Mississippi, where her family had owned land and a general store, to St. Louis, where they'd bought property, and where her husband's mother and aunt's sister had respectable jobs in service. She had taught school in Mississippi; she learned dressmaking in St. Louis. She took a second husband, an attractive, well-spoken man from a respectable colored family, and together they moved to Chicago for better jobs and more independence.

The St. Louis dressmaker became a Chicago dressmaker with well-to-do white clients at the posh Edgewater Beach Hotel. (The beach was private and patrons were often flown there by helicopter.)

Lily McClendon Armstrong became *Lillian* McClendon Armstrong in Chicago. The additional syllable was appropriate for worldlier Northern ears. The St. Louis husband was left behind when, after several years, he continued to show insufficient ambition.

All politics are local, and when she turned her attention to politics she entered at a very local level, collecting votes door-to-door for a Negro precinct captain in the Democratic Party. She always delivered a high count, so he made her a playground supervisor, which she found benevolently dull. With the party's support, she became one of Chicago's first Negro policewomen. This she enjoyed.

"Lemme go with you, babe," said a drunken man one night when she was out of uniform and on her way home. "Certainly" came her genial reply, whereupon she asked him into her car and drove him to the police station.

She was courted by a doctor, an older man, whose children,

she felt, were possessive and unwelcoming. She stepped out with a dashing aviator who fought with Haile Selassie's army in World War II. Her third husband was a Pullman porter, a stolid, amiable man who followed her lead as she studied property values, and contributed his earnings to their real estate fund. When he died, she owned two buildings. Every week, tenants placed their rent in the courteous, peremptory hand of Lillian McClendon Armstrong Thompson.

Dowagers of color fitted themselves out in suits and furs, gloves and well-fixed hats—the cloche, toque, beret and turban, the pillbox, the angled brim.

When walking sticks were in fashion, Lillian McClendon Armstrong carried one with an ivory handle.

When she bought her first mink coat some years later, she wore it down to St. Louis to visit family. "Mother," said her teenage daughter, "it's too hot for fur."

"It's never too hot for fur," Lillian McClendon Armstrong Thompson answered, and set off on her trip.

I remember my grandmother and her friends in woolen suits and fox pelts with head and feet; pants suits and silk shirtwaists; crisp hats with half veils.

When their daughters were in their eighties, they still quoted their mother's pronouncements.

If you ever get pregnant, don't bother to stop by the house. Just keep walking east. (To the lake.)

And:

When I left my husband I left him his easy chair. I knew it was the only piece of furniture he couldn't do without.

Dowagers of color saw their daughters through college, even

graduate school, and into good marriages with lawyers, doctors, educators, journalists, accountants, post office supervisors, and businessmen. They made sure that their girls had equal access to the responsible ways and winning manners they needed to make a good marriage.

After decades of marital and monetary protection, these daughters took on their mothers' astringency. Once they were widowed they chose to remain so. One outlived two suave and charming companions, neither of whom she married, both of whom she inherited money from. Another outlived the worldly judge who'd escorted her to prestigious cultural events and parties.

Widowers on the prowl were entertained with watchful efficiency, their movements reported by phone or at club meetings.

Mrs. G.: "One gentleman made his rounds testing their cooking, and testing his welcome. Gloria tolerated him till he started placing orders. Then he came to me. I told him, 'I'm looking for the same thing you are: a home-cooked meal from somebody else's home.'"

Elderly single men were not randomly encouraged. "That's a lovely perfume you're wearing," said one when Mrs. S. entered the elevator of their building one afternoon. She packed her answer into a nod and a brisk fib. "Thank you, but I don't wear perfume."

Because my paternal grandmother lived in California, I didn't know her nearly as well. She taught elementary school in Mississippi and took in laundry and sewed. She was a seamstress and an avid union member in California; in her early years there she worked as a dressmaker's fitter for at least one Hollywood studio. Her husband was a master carpenter; her four children, she decreed, were to be doctors, lawyers, or—in the case of the daughter—a teacher. Of the three sons, two become lawyers, then judges, and one became a doctor. The daughter then acquired not one, not two, but three master's degrees. One to match each brother's achievement.

A Retelling: The Daughter Who Became My Mother

My mother did not have the impressive sewing skills of her mother or her mother-in-law. She could mend a torn hem and sew on buttons. And this had been my ambitious grandmother's plan. Irma was not allowed to scrub floors (other household duties, yes, but no scrubbing of floors). Irma was to graduate from the University of Chicago. (There wasn't enough money for four years there, so she transferred in.) Irma was taught to look for quality when she shopped; she could shop more once she'd married well; she could have her own seamstress or dressmaker.

And my mother loved to shop, for herself, and for us: she delighted in her wardrobe. When she turned ninety-two and was getting dressed for her birthday club's luncheon, I asked what her favorite clothes had been. I expected total recall of millinery triumphs in sisal or felt. (I still remember a Tastee Freez swirl of a hat from the early sixties, cream-colored with a black veil.) But she chose her evening dresses.

"Short or long?"

"Both."

"What was the difference?"

"The short ones were flip and flirty."

"And the long ones?"

She laughed and put one hand to her forehead, fingers arranged in a classic heroine-about-to-swoon pose. "Beware, my foolish heart," she drawled.

> The night is like a lovely tune,
> Beware, my foolish heart . . .

That ballad appeared in 1949, when my mother was thirty-three and I was two. I like to imagine my parents moving onto the dance floor as Willie Randall's orchestra took a sumptuous plunge into its opening notes.

"My Foolish Heart," "Lush Life," "Stardust," "Misty," "Sophisticated Lady" . . . I heard these songs over and over on our record player. The flip and flirty numbers too, deft syncopations of wit, lust, and romance. "That Old Black Magic," "Do Nothing Till You Hear from Me," "Gee Baby, Ain't I Good to You?" And of course that urbane salty blues which hailed our city:

> Goin' to Chicago,
> Sorry but I can't take you.

Those proud Chicago department stores where we shopped! Marshall Field and Chas. A. Stevens, designed by the firm of D. H. Burnham, the architect who'd ruled the World's Fair. Carson, Pirie, Scott, designed by Louis B. Sullivan, master builder of the skyscraper. Mighty structures of granite and terra-cotta; arrogantly eclectic with their escalators and Tiffany lamps, their modernist lines and Renaissance flourishes. They sat in the city's commercial center, the downtown Loop, flanked by hotels, theaters, and office buildings. Proclaiming the union of exclusivity and accessibility. These late-nineteenth- and early-twentieth-century department stores were the first to make sensory bombardment a stately art.

Counter after counter of lipsticks, powders, perfumes; cases filled with gloves (wrist-length, mid-arm, lined, unlined, cotton, suede, kid, white, cream, black, tan), leather goods, candies—and we haven't even reached the escalators. We're still on the ground floor, which stretches across two city blocks.

For girls like my sister and me, "shopping" was an intricately plotted expedition. Our mother was the guide. She showed us what to look for, as our eyes wandered and wondered. She showed us what to pass by. *She* directed the gaze.

Marshall Field, where our mother took us to sit on Santa's knee at Christmas in a maze of giant wreaths, candy canes, and glazed whirling ornaments.

Marshall Field, where our mother took us to lunch at the Walnut Room.

Marshall Field's 28 Shop, where Mother told her mother, "You really shouldn't smoke here," and her mother answered, "As much as I pay for these clothes, I'll do what I want."

Marshall Field, where my father's aunt Nancy passed for white to work as a saleswoman in the 1920s.

At Saks and Bonwit Teller the exclusivity-accessibility balance shifted. They were smaller, more discreet stores. They were on the posh Near North Side, not in the "come hither all ye consumers" Loop. The rhythm of buying and selling was more decorous, the conversation quieter. And you knew when you entered that fewer people felt they could take the liberty—claim the right—to walk through as tourists. Mother didn't take us there before 1960. As Negroes we had to secure our place down-town before we ventured north toward the Gold Coast.

Every month a coffee-table-sized *Vogue* arrived at our house. Every month I devoured it. The models were starting to be known by name. My favorite was red-haired Suzy Parker: tall and lissome; her face a perfect assemblage of curves (the lips, the eyebrows) and lines (the nose, the cheekbones). The models wore the grand European designs of Dior, Givenchy, Balenciaga, and Madame Grès. They showed off the clothes of Americans with rhythmically neat or alliterative names: Geoffrey Beene, Bill Blass, Norman Norell. They were muses and fetish objects, offerings on the altar of feminine glamour.

And I worshipped offerings to feminine glamour, in maga-zines, in movies, and in life. The clothes; the lingerie; the array of handkerchiefs, some lace-trimmed, some initialed; pocket-books of leather and alligator, bearing their own mirrors and coin purses; peau de soie clutch bags for evening or small beaded ones with handles that just slipped over your wrist. The perfume and cologne bottles on Mama's vanity dresser. The ear-rings, bracelets, necklaces, arranged in the leather jewelry box with its Florentine design.

I learned to accept the verbotens too. One summer day I came downstairs wearing a red blouse and a purple and white flowered skirt; I was sent right back up to change. You don't wear certain colors together, especially loud colors. Denim is only for weekend play and summer camp. Little girls don't wear nail polish. Little girls wear *white* socks with their Mary Janes.

I accepted the verbotens because I longed to be a perfect girl, and if a girl lacked perfect prettiness—which I did—then this

was a route to compensatory perfection. I accepted the verbotens because they came from my mother, whose appearance and
manner I found both authoritative and deeply pleasing. Her
crisp Claudette Colbert hairdo; her five-foot-three-inch frame,
trim and shapely but not skinny; her smooth beige-brown skin.
She was witty, lively, and chic. So were her friends. I loved how
they looked in their suits and silk shirtwaists, their furs and
smart hats. I loved how they carried themselves at luncheons
and parties. I loved the quick comments and judgments they
flung out. They were in feminine command.

And they were almost entirely absent from the main stage
of feminine glamour, from *Vogue,* from *Harper's Bazaar,* from
Life and *Look,* from television, from movies. (Call up the usual
exceptions: Lena, Dorothy, Eartha, Diahann.) Race had decreed
it so.

How did I register the fact that everyone who mattered in
this vast beauty-and-fashion complex was white? Not until the
1960s did models of color start appearing. Headline, 1962: Gordon Parks—a Negro himself, who photographed my mother
and her friends at the South Side Community Arts Center in
the thirties—shoots a *Life* spread on "exotic" clothes, titled
"Swirl of Bright Hues: New Styles Shown by Negro Models—
A Band of Beautiful Pioneers." Headline, 1966: Donyale Luna,
who describes herself as Irish, Mexican, and Afro-Egyptian,
becomes the first Negro model to make the cover of *Vogue.* Her
fingers were long, tapering, distinctly red-brown. Her nails were
colored shell-white. Her second and third fingers framed one
dark eye in a curved but unmistakable V; that dark orb of an
eye, lined Egyptian-cat style, commanded homage.

Who among us could look like that? She was as anomalous as
Suzy Parker. But she was our anomaly. She let us feel possessive
and vindicated.

The fashion and beauty complex has so many ways to enchant and maim. It invents styles and standards that create impossible longings. If you're smitten, your cravings start early. You want something—some feature, some body part, some look or aura—you do not have and will not ever have.

Those cheekbones, which make the thought of a skull
    erotic;
Those rosebud lips, so sweetly small;
That sleek neck, that long torso, those lean, kinetic sculpture legs.

Begin with those biological impossibilities. Then add racial ones:

The delicate whimsy of Audrey Hepburn.
The sultry lushness of Elizabeth Taylor.
The country club sangfroid of Grace Kelly.

No! You cannot ever be white like these idols of feminine perfection. Let that final impossibility reproach and taunt you.

Nevertheless, a separate world of Negro beauty and glamour did exist when *Ebony* arrived. Every month I studied its cream, beige, tan, buff, brown, and sepia models. My favorite was Dorothea Towles. She was just six years younger than our mother, who'd met her. She'd gone to college, as we were to do; she'd married a dentist (we were supposed to marry professionals); she'd decided to follow her sister, a serious concert pianist, to Paris. And once there she'd broken ranks to fulfill our wild secret fantasies of Josephine Baker crossed with Audrey Hepburn: she'd gone to the house of Dior, become a model, and gone from Dior to Schiaparelli and Balmain.

I admired her, I envied her, but I didn't worship her as I worshipped Suzy Parker. She was in *Ebony*, not *Vogue*. My white friends didn't know who she was. Diana Vreeland didn't have to know or care.

When I look at pictures of Dorothea now, I realize just how adorable she was. She had the kinetic sculpture legs, the sleek neck and shoulders.

I say "adorable" because her face was piquant. The high cheekbones were there, but their shape was softly round (like Baker's). The full lower lip was there, the pouty lip that would be so desirable in the 1960s and '70s. Her dark eyes had a playful, almost quizzical expression, as if she were amused to watch the world watch her. Her hair was dark too—except when she chose to dye it blonde.

Did she turn her back on her people? She did not. Did she return to bourgeois obscurity as a dentist's wife? Not that either. She did return to the United States in 1954, and she did leave her husband for good. Then, using her own numerous haute couture clothes, she barnstormed the country, organizing all-black fashion shows for all-black sororities and charities.

Jet loved to chronicle her flamboyant doings, enhanced by photos. "Model Dorothea Towles created a sensation when she strolled into a white fur shop in Birmingham and asked to rent $10,000 worth of furs for the Alpha Kappa Alpha's fashion show. The owner sent along three private cops to guard the furs." This next to a picture of pert, carefree Towles at the beach, perched on a rock in a two-piece strapless bathing suit, high-heeled ankle-strap sandals, and a wide, fringed straw hat.

Dorothea Towles had returned to America the year the Supreme Court decreed segregation illegal in public schools. Separate but equal was being challenged everywhere. And four years later Dorothea's fashion challenge was taken up by my mother's friend Eunice Johnson. Her husband, John Johnson, published *Ebony, Jet,* and *Negro Digest.* She'd given *Ebony* its bold, pre–Black Power name; she'd become the company's secretary-treasurer and aesthetic adviser. Now she launched the Ebony Fashion Fair, a touring fashion show on a grander scale.

She didn't need to use her own clothes. She'd go to the top shows in Paris and Milan, sit in front-row seats beside white editors, and buy clothes. She'd go to the top shows in New York, sit in front-row seats beside white editors, and buy clothes. She'd go in search of young black designers and buy clothes. Beige, tan, buff, cream, sepia, brown, and (eventually) ebony models strode and sashayed down hotel runways in city after city, wearing these clothes for colored/Negro/black and African-American audiences at white hotels. It was spectacular.

We were still separate, but separate *and* equal was always Negroland's de facto social motto. We were still not wholly equal, of course. The white world had made the rules that excluded us; now, when it saw fit, it altered those rules to include *a few* of us. Politics was changing the culture and the market: the aesthetics of fashion and glamour were changing too. But we had been there all along. Before they noticed or acknowledged us, we were there.

I often look through the clothes my mother has given me through the years. I cherish the Pauline Trigère brushed-wool, funnel-shaped coat, beige with thin stripes of pale mauve, lilac, blue, and white. Such quiet symmetry it could be wallpaper. I feel like a craft object when I close my body into this coat. And I feel vindicated too, because Pauline Trigère was the first top

American designer to use a black model regularly. We *always* knew these things; *Ebony, Jet,* or our mothers told us.

Still, the piece I most love wearing is Mother's gold brocade cocktail dress with matching jacket. It was designed by Malcolm Starr, known for bejeweled sixties evening wear. The dress is sleeveless, with wide straps, a nipped waist, and a wraparound-style skirt. Not a wide skirt, but wide enough for a feminist to walk in without mincing her steps. The waist-length jacket is trimmed in gold braid; so is the skirt's front panel.

It's "flip and flirty," as my mother prescribed. It's crisp yet splendid. It makes me feel I've put on made-to-order armor.

My mother's armor.

Armor that helped shield me from exclusion.

Armor that helped shield me from inferiority.

I believe it's too easy to recount unhappy memories when you write about yourself. You bask in your own innocence. You revere your grief. You arrange your angers at their most becoming angles.

I don't want this kind of indulgence to dominate my memories. So let me try to describe some varieties of my experience one last time.

When race is simply there and "Negroes" are your familiars, their faces, voices, bodies are the landscape of your everyday life. The shock comes when a person appears from that other, wider world; when an action, a fact, an event suddenly marks you as the oddity, the marred feature of a landscape. You, your people: the singular is turned undesirably plural. You're ambushed: literally and violently, *taken aback*. That's unhappiness. That's outrage. That's . . . grief.

Then there are those other kinds of racial shocks: ecstatic recognitions; sudden terror. Race is not simply there; instead, you and your people have a charged destiny. You, the singular made uncannily plural, have been seized and placed in the center of world attention. You and your people don't share just a past, you share looks and gestures, ways of talking, moving, being, that others everywhere revile, covet, debate.

How do you adapt your singular, willful self to so much history and myth? So much glory, banality, honor, and betrayal?

———

But at least race mattered when I was growing up. At least it enflamed the nation. Gender didn't. No one who directed the Big Cultural Conversations—political leaders, influential artists, journalists—none of them made that claim for gender. Not blatantly, not commandingly, Equal rights for women tucked itself into those ladylike organizations—the League of Women Voters, the National Council of Negro Women, Planned Parenthood—that did good work in politics, social service, and public health. I should say "good *works*" to convey their aura of worthy, conscientious dullness. If you'd bothered to look at these organizations, you'd have found a vigorous, even contentious feminist past. In our 1950s and '60s present, they looked like the pious Victorians we had no intention of being.

Society met the idea of women fighting for equality with mockery, contempt, or repressive tolerance. When a senator from Virginia attached to the Voting Rights Act of 1964 a clause prohibiting sex discrimination, liberals were outraged. They (we) accused him of racist manipulation, since most senators could be counted on to defeat any bill with that provision; and they (we) denounced him for ridiculing the bill since women's rights were so trivial compared to Negroes'. Now the contradictory reasoning is obvious, but then we didn't notice or care. Few, if any, girls my age knew, and few of our mothers and grandmothers saw, that we'd just been trapped again in that fierce and ugly nineteenth-century quarrel about the Fifteenth Amendment, a quarrel that would soon become a fierce and ugly late-twentieth-century struggle about the relative importance of black rights (dominated by men) and women's rights (dominated by whites).

Whatever our race, girls of my generation with economic and cultural security took certain rights for granted. Not rights, no—these were privileges, and they varied according to your family and environment. In mine the privileges were good schooling and cultural enrichment to make you well rounded, develop your taste and charm.

You were to be distinctive and outstanding.

You were *not* to be disruptive.

You were to reflect your world at its ordered best, its gender-ordered best.

Education and cultivation would enhance, hopefully ensure, your ability to attract eligible boys and men. Which meant economic security and social status. Negro mothers did make a point of warning their daughters to "have a career you can fall back on": economic security was always less secure for Negro husbands and fathers.

But even if your career ambitions far exceeded "something to fall back on," they were not to be sundered from that generic female future. Every professional woman I knew was a wife, and most were mothers too. Some teachers were exceptions, but they'd better be young and cool if they hoped to avoid the "spinster! lesbian!" tee-hees of students.

And out in the wide wide world, the famous women we gazed upon never stopped reminding us that we must cherish that generic female future. Especially the artistic, glamorous ones. It wasn't just the movies and plays they starred in or the music they sang. It was the incessant interviews they gave to newspapers, magazines, television reporters. In interview after interview, women celebrities would flaunt their families or their dreams of family. Yes, success was fine, even thrilling, they'd say—or be quoted as saying—but really, nothing mattered more than their children, or the children they hoped to have. What could all their success mean, they'd muse, without the right man to love and come home to? And if they had no children and clearly weren't going to, *that* became the great regret of their life. So went the cultural trade-off: the few women who'd won acclaim and a certain power were expected to prove their loyalty to the status quo. No doubt some of them believed it. No doubt some of them thought they should believe it and tried to believe it. No doubt all of them knew it was good, even essential for their public image.

In secret, marriage and motherhood felt drab to me (and, we now know, to millions of girls like and not like me). Drab, stomach-churning, and gloom-bringing. Because really, whatever your race or ethnicity, you knew that if your girl skills weren't up to par, your intelligence/education/talent would become a liability—proof that your proportions were off, that you were excessive or insufficient.

Work. Excel.

But learn to flirt, tease, date. Every boy is good practice.

We weren't fools. Even in high school girls resented certain dating rituals and assumptions, found little ways to thwart them. But we didn't treat them as part of a system, a structure, a politics. Not until the women's movement took hold of us (of me), in 1969 and '70, and cast its light backwards, on all we'd done and not done, did we see the whole.

In my childhood, it seemed to me that my world of mothers and daughters contained everything anyone could need. But of course the strictures and prohibitions were there, cued up, ready to play. "I hate boys or I hate ———" (whoever had beaten you in some game), you'd crow to your mother's friends, then stand there, feeling silly when they exchanged looks and cooed back: "You'll grow out of that soon enough."

Maybe the disparity started with physical competition. I wasn't a tomboy. But I didn't like it that boys thought we couldn't beat them at sports when we beat them at other things. And when puberty hurled its gonadotropins our way, the few girls who'd always played soccer and baseball with boys and sometimes beat them got shut out. Shut out by the boys; looked down on by sports-deriding girls they were supposed to start being friends with.

For me, the worst was trying to master the special effects of boy-girl pursuit. It was grueling. Hint, then declare; confess, prevaricate; have power, yield control—all the while trying to protect your tenuous sense of self. It was maddening, this business of playing shallow, acting giddier than you were. My sister had the strongest will of anyone I knew. But in the company of boys she'd make her voice higher and softer, become more obliging. Then, the boy gone, she'd switch right back into mastery mode. And my brainy, sharp-tongued best friend. "How will I know what to think if I don't know what he thinks?" she asked her diary after a high school date with a sweet, quiet, and handsome boy. Some years later it struck her that he may have had no thoughts to express.

Thenthenthenthen . . . lurking or imposing itself, stirring and wearying you: the perpetual question of The Negro Woman. Her history of struggle, degradation, triumph; her exclusion from the rewards of bourgeois femininity; *her duty to strengthen the Negro family.* Not a history one wanted to haul through one's social life. Not a history one wanted to lumber into the sexual revolution with. Not a history one wanted to have sternly codified by white sociologists and Black Power revolutionaries who found the faults of The Black Woman much the same as those of The Negro Woman. She was bellicose, she was self-centered; she was sexually prudish when not castrating.

The solution: Black Woman, concur, submit, and improve your attitude!

Florynce Kennedy was the first black feminist I saw in public and in action. Lawyer, protester, organizer, she was born in 1916, the same year as my mother—and four years before women of any color got the vote. A whiplash tongue and a cowboy hat; suede and leather pants (am I imagining that she sometimes wore chaps?); dangling earrings and many necklaces (some with women's rights symbols, some with bright stones and feathers). She was tall and fabulously grandstanding. She'd planted herself and thrived in every movement that counted: civil rights, anti-war, black power, feminism, gay rights. Her principles never swerved; her tactics never staled. She used to say something like this:

When black women tell me feminism is a white woman's thing, I tell them: you've spent all these years, all these centuries, imitating every bad idea white women came up with—about their hair, their makeup, their clothes, their duties to their men. And now, they finally come up with one good idea—feminism—and you decide you don't want anything to do with it!

Civil rights. The New Left. Black Power. Feminism. Gay rights. To be remade so many times in one generation is surely a blessing.

So I won't trap myself into quantifying which matters more, race, or gender, or class. Race, gender, and class are basic elements of one's living. Basic as utensils and clothing; always in use; always needing repairs and updates. Basic as body and breath, justice and reason, passion and imagination. So the question isn't "Which matters most?," it's "How does each matter?" Gender, race, class; class, race, gender—your three in one and one in three.

Being an Other, in America, teaches you to imagine what can't imagine you. That's your first education. Then comes the second. Call it your social and intellectual change. The world outside you gets reconfigured, and inside too. Patterns deviate and fracture. Hierarchies disperse. Now you can imagine yourself as central. It feels grand. But don't stop there. Let that self extend into other narratives and truths.

All of them shifting even as I write.

Don't let me end in the realm of lilting abstraction. It comes down to this: Am I someone whose character and behavior do not hold the world back in these ways? Have I made a viable life for myself?

An adult life takes shape. You (me) are a writer, a journalist, a critic. You are a woman who grew up as a Negro and usually calls herself black. ("African American" is strictly for official discourse.) Genealogically speaking, you are of African, Irish, English, and Indian descent.

You are a single woman; you intend to remain one. You've acquired enough sexual experience to feel you belong to your times. You do not have children; you never intended to. Sustained romantic intensities have not been for you. Your explanation (not an untrue one, though not quite sufficient) is that you have let yourself be shaped by so many conventions, expectations, and requirements (institutions', people's), by so much dread of disapproval, that the discipline of solitude—severe solitude—has been required to give you the sense of an independent selfhood. The intensities of friendship suit you better.

Friendship's choreography is for multiple partners: for varied groups and surprisingly sustained duets.

"The human psyche is pathetic," I say—I declaim—to my psychopharmacologist.

"It's what we have, Miss Jefferson," he replies, "it's what we have."

And what I have is what I take to my psychotherapist each week. What I have is what we make together, each supplying the material she knows best.

There are days when I still want to dismantle this constructed self of mine. You did it so badly, I think. You lost so much time. And then I tell myself, so what?

So what?

Go on.

Acknowledgments

This book would not exist without a much-loved family of friends who spurred me to write, think, and persevere: Lynn Jones Barbour, Alexandra Chasin, Susan Dickler, Ann Douglas, Wendy Gimbel, Sophia Hall, Anthony Heilbut, Laura Karp, Adrienne Kennedy, Jo Lang, Betty Shamieh, Betty Ann Solinger, Laurie Stone, and Wendy Walters. Special thanks to friends Elizabeth Kendall, irreplaceable first reader, and Charlotte Carter, impeccable first copy editor.

Parts of this book were published, in different forms, in *Bookforum, MORE, The Believer, Guernica, The Inevitable: Contemporary Writers Confront Death,* and *What My Mother Gave Me: Thirty-one Women on the Gifts That Mattered Most.* I am grateful to the editors.

I was enormously helped by a grant from the John Simon Guggenheim Memorial Foundation, and stimulated by the company of colleagues and friends at Columbia University, especially that of Phillip Lopate, guardian of the essay in all its forms.

Many of my family's Chicago friends are gone. I salute their graceful ghosts and honor those living, particularly Sue Barnett Ish, Wyonella Smith, the Northeasterners, and the Birthday Club members. St. Edmund's Episcopal Church and its rector, Richard L. Tolliver, were bulwarks for my parents; additional thanks to Father David Stanford and Cheryl A. Harris for their kindness to my mother in her last years. Mary Willis and Jacqueline Blakely were crucial to her well-being and to mine. I will never forget their kindness.

It's been a pleasure and honor to work again with my editor at Pantheon, Erroll McDonald, and with my agent, Sarah Chalfant. Thanks to Ellen Feldman, my scrupulous production editor; Nicholas Latimer, my ebullient photographer; Josie Kals, whose attention never flagged; and the rest of the Pantheon staff. Oliver Munday's jacket design was perfection.

Finally, loving gratitude to my niece, Francesca Harper, who shared her memories, her humor, her photographs, and the company of her husband, Eric Cohen, and their daughter, Harper Io Denise Cohen.

Notes

11 "to see my race lifted": Frances Jackson Coppin quoted in *We Are Your Sisters: Black Women in the Nineteenth Century,* ed. Dorothy Sterling (New York: W. W. Norton, 1984), 205.

13 "the lighter accomplishments": Joseph Willson, *The Elite of Our People: Joseph Willson's Sketches of Black Upper-Class Life in Antebellum Philadelphia,* ed. Julie Winch (State College: Pennsylvania State University Press, 2000), 89.

13 "You have seen how a man": Frederick Douglass, *The Narrative and Selected Writings,* ed. Michael Meyer (New York: Modern Library College Edmons, 1983), 75.

14 "on account of her care and attention": Willson, *The Elite of Our People,* 52.

14 "suitable household and Kitchen furniture": Ibid., 54.

15 "undoubtedly excite the mirth": Ibid., 79.

16 "The prejudiced world has for a long time": Ibid., 97.

16 "that portion of colored society": Ibid., 87.

17 "The machinery of the watch": Ibid., 88.

18 "in the manner of suitors": Ibid., 103.

18 In fact, after receiving a small number: Ibid., 48–49.

18 "Fred. Douglass and his able compatriots": Cyprian Clamorgan, *The Colored Aristocracy of St. Louis,* ed. Julie Winch (Columbia: University of Missouri Press, 1999), 45–46.

19 "tonsorial profession": Ibid., 52.

19 "separated from the white race": Ibid., 45.

20 "If the reader will accompany me": Ibid., 48.

20 "Mrs. Rutgers is an illiterate woman": Ibid., 49.

20 "and is good for one hundred thousand dollars": Ibid., 51.

20 "Not so bad a speculation": Ibid., 55.

20 "is a good man": Ibid., 60.

20 "They are both no doubt sorry": Ibid., 60–61.

21   "rather dilapidated": Ibid., 60.

21   "can command the cool sum": Ibid., 59.

21   "will startle many of our white friends": Ibid., 63.

21   "the result of the unwearied and combined action": Ibid., 47.

24   "On the wharf was a motley assemblage": Charlotte Forten Grimké, *The Journals of Charlotte Forten Grimké,* ed. Brenda Stevenson, Schomburg Library of Nineteenth-Century Black Women Writers (New York: Oxford University Press, 1988), 388–89.

24   "I wonder that every colored person": Ibid., 140.

25   "I will pray that God": Ibid., 376.

25   "full of the shouting spirit": Ibid., 402.

25   "These people have really a great deal": Charlotte Forten quoted in *We Are Your Sisters,* pp. 281, 510n.

26   "that noblest of compensations": Ibid., 284.

28   "to promote social intercourse": Willson, *The Elite of Our People,* 68.

30   "for almost any offense": Ida B. Wells-Barnett, *The Red Record: Tabulated Statistics and Alleged Causes of Lynching in the United States* (Guttenberg eBook, 2005), chapter 1.

30   "The Southern white man says": Ibid.

31   "linked with that of every agony": Anna Julia Cooper, *A Voice from the South,* Schomburg Library of Nineteenth-Century Black Women Writers (New York: Oxford University Press, 1988), 122.

32   "such new and alluring vistas": Ibid., 143–44.

32   "the lowly, the illiterate": Mary Church Terrell quoted in Mary Helen Washington, introduction to Cooper, *A Voice from the South,* xxx.

33   "Does any race produce more": W. E. B. Du Bois quoted in David Levering Lewis, *W. E. B. Du Bois: Biography of a Race, 1868–1919* (New York: Henry Holt, 1993), 288.

33   "the only Southern book": Henry James quoted ibid., 277.

34   "a willingness to sacrifice and plan": W. E. B. Du Bois, "The Talented Tenth Memorial Address," *Boulé Journal* (1948), in *W. E. B. Du Bois: A Reader,* ed. David Levering Lewis (New York: Henry Holt, 1995), 350.

34   "a group of selfish, self-indulgent": Ibid., 349.

35   "pathological struggle for status": E. Franklin Frazier, *Black Bourgeoisie* (New York: Free Press, 1997), 212.

35   "It appears that middle-class Negroes": Ibid., 1.

36   "I have lived it for over eighty years": Gerri Major with Doris Saunders, *Black Society* (Chicago: Johnson Publishing, 1976), vii.

37 "exclusive" and "prestigious" schools: Lawrence Otis Graham, *Our Kind of People: Inside America's Black Upper Class* (New York: Harper Perennial, 2000).

38 "Virtually all Negro field artillery officers": Major Welton I. Taylor with Karyn J. Taylor, *Two Steps from Glory: A World War II Liaison Pilot Confronts Jim Crow and the Enemy in the South Pacific* (Winning Strategy Press, 2012), 45.

44 *Humor is laughing at what you haven't got:* Langston Hughes, "A Note on Humor," from *The Book of Negro Humor,* in *The Collected Works of Langston Hughes: Essays on Art, Race, Politics, and World Affairs,* ed. Christopher C. De Santis (Columbia: University of Missouri Press, 2002), 525.

64 "You've got to be taught to be afraid": Richard Rodgers and Oscar Hammerstein II, "You've Got to Be Carefully Taught," *South Pacific* (1949).

67 "Blow out the candle": Phil Moore, "Blow Out the Candle."

68 "While tearing off a game of golf": Cole Porter, "My Heart Belongs to Daddy."

69 "I'm here to tell you": Clyde Lovern Otis and Murray Stein, "Smooth Operator (Mercy Mister Percy)."

75 "Sherman Billingsley cooks for me": June Carroll and Arthur Siegel, "Monotonous," *New Faces of 1952.*

79 "The child, not the lesson": John Dewey, *The School and Society,* quoted in William Harms and Ida DePencier, *100 Years of Learning at The University of Chicago Laboratory Schools* (1996), www.ucls.uchicago .edu/about-lab/current-publications/history/index/aspx.

83 "The question of the child's future": James Weldon Johnson, *Along This Way* (New York: Penguin, 1990), 56.

85 "The thousand injuries of Caucasians": Edgar Allan Poe, "The Cask of Amontillado"; my alteration.

85 "A wrong is unredressed": Ibid.

101 *"Stitch Stitch Stitch":* Thomas Hood, "Song of the Shirt," in *Adventures in English Literature,* ed. R. B. Inglis et al. (Toronto: W. J. Gage, 1952), 436–37.

101 "He weeps by the side of the ocean": Edward Lear, "How Pleasant to Know Mr. Lear," quoted in John Lehmann, *Edward Lear and His World* (New York: Scribner's, 1977), 116.

102 "Well, son, I'll tell you": Langston Hughes, "Mother to Son," in *The*

Collected Poems of Langston Hughes, ed. Arnold Rampersad (New York: Alfred A. Knopf, 1994), 30.

121   *The secret signal:* Virginia Woolf, *Mrs. Dalloway* (New York: Harcourt, 1981), 88.

124   "Fat black bucks": Vachel Lindsay, "The Congo," in *American Poetry: Twentieth Century,* vol. 1 (New York: Library of America, 2000), 215–77.

126   "Boom, kill the white men": Ibid., 276.

126   "they all repented": Ibid., 278.

127   " 'Mumbo . . . Jumbo' ": Ibid., 280.

131   "Gr-r-r—there go": Robert Browning, "Soliloquy of the Spanish Cloister," in *Victorian Verse,* ed. George MacBeth (New York, Penguin, 1969), 102–4.

140   "The story of the Negro in America": James Baldwin, *Notes of a Native Son,* in *Baldwin: Collected Essays,* ed. Toni Morrison (New York: Library of America, 1998), 19.

141   "One may say that the Negro in America": Ibid.

141   "The ways in which the Negro": Ibid.

142   "We cannot ask": Ibid.

142   "This world is white no longer": Ibid., 129.

143   "*Uncle Tom's Cabin* is a very bad novel": Ibid., 11–12.

169   *Awaiting each colored child:* Johnson, *Along This Way,* 56.

172   "I am a black woman": "Mari Evans, *I Am a Black Woman* (New York: Morrow, 1970), n.p.

174   *good-looking in a boring way:* Adrienne Kennedy, *Funnyhouse of a Negro,* in *The Adrienne Kennedy Reader* (Minneapolis: University of Minnesota Press, 2001), 14–15.

174   "The poor bitch": Ibid., 25.

176   "Thief!" Sexton wrote: Anne Sexton, "Sylvia's Death," in *The Complete Poems* (New York: Mariner, 1999), 126.

178   "You don't know what love is": Don Raye and Gene de Paul, "You Don't Know What Love Is."

178   *I cry your mercy:* John Keats, "I cry your mercy," in *The Poems of John Keats,* ed. H. W. Garrod (Oxford: Oxford University Press, 1958), 371.

179   *Every day a little death:* Stephen Sondheim, "Every Day a Little Death," from *A Little Night Music,* 1997.

179   "A sense of incalculable past loss and injury": Frances Anne Kemble,

Journal of a Residence on a Georgian Plantation in 1838–1839 (1863; Cambridge: Cambridge University Press, 2009), 122.

179 "I think this journal will be disadvantageous": Mary Boykin Chestnut, *A Diary from Dixie,* ed. Ben Ames Williams (Cambridge, Mass.: Harvard University Press, 1980), 22.

180 "I had wanted to compromise with Fate": Charlotte Brontë, *Villette* (New York: Harper Colophon, 1972), 222.

180 "I sometimes wish that I could fall": Harriet A. Jacobs, *Incidents in the Life of a Slave Girl,* ed. Jean Fagan Yellin (Cambridge, Mass.: Harvard University Press, 1987), 238.

180 "You are you": Elizabeth Bishop, "The Country Mouse," in *The Collected Prose* (New York: Noonday Press, 1993), 33.

181 "My hand is stuffed": Gwendolyn Brooks, "The Children of the Poor," in *Selected Poems* (New York: Harper & Row, 1963), 53.

181 "Plunge ahead": Jamaica Kincaid, *See Now Then* (New York: Farrar, Straus and Giroux, 2014), 91–92.

181 "I have stories to tell?": Wendy Walters, "A Letter from the Hunted in Retrospect," in *Longer I Wait, More You Love Me: Poems* (Berkeley, Calif.: Palm Press, 2009), 30.

182 "in the drifting community": Rachel Carson, "The Edge of the Sea," in *Lost Woods: The Discovered Writing of Rachel Carson,* ed. Linda Lear (Boston: Beacon Press, 1998), 139.

185 "If there be anything like a colored lady": Charlotte Hawkins Brown, quoted in Charles W. Wadlington and Richard F. Knapp, *Charlotte Hawkins Brown and Palmer Memorial Institute* (Chapel Hill: University of North Carolina Press, 1999), 16.

187 "What kind of pictures do we select": Quoted in Deborah Gray White, *Too Heavy a Load: Black Women in Defense of Themselves, 1894–1994* (New York: W. W. Norton, 1999), 74.

187 *Buy mother a box of handkerchiefs:* Charlotte Hawkins Brown, *"Mammy": An Appeal to the Heart of the South; The Correct Thing To Do—To Say—To Wear* (Boston: G. K. Hall, 1995), 5, 10, 33, 46, 77.

188 "Dear Friend": Ibid., 33.

188 "To Do and to Say": Ibid., 37, 110, 43, 114.

188 "If you go to the dining car": Ibid., 119.

189 "Do not go to buy a hat": Ibid., 95, 33.

189 "calm and undisturbed soul": Ibid., 106.

190 "too familiar" on a bus or train: Ibid., 84.

190   *"in her own way":* Ibid., vii.

190   "The arrangement of one's hair": Ibid., 43.

190   "Ain't I a woman": Sojourner Truth, Speech at the Women's Rights Convention, Akron, Ohio, May 28–29, 1851.

210   " 'It's so dreadful to be poor!' ": Louisa May Alcott, *Little Women,* in *Alcott: Little Women, Little Men, Jo's Boys,* ed. Elaine Showalter (New York: Library of America, 2005), 7.

211   "You are old enough": Ibid., 9.

211   "As for you, Amy": Ibid.

213   "An old maid": Ibid., 466.

213   "one can get on quite happily": Ibid.

214   "Don't laugh at the spinsters": Ibid., 466–67.

215   "a handsome feature in his face": Ibid., 355.

215   "nearly setting the chimney afire": Ibid., 378.

215   "pity from your heart": Ibid.

216   "wilderness of boys": Ibid., 509.

216   "Christmas won't be Christmas": Ibid., 7.

216   "We don't cheat in America": Ibid., 135.

217   "Birds in their little nests": Ibid., 9.

217   "But when I saw you all so well": Ibid., 397.

217   "She could not say": Ibid., 398.

219   "without mispronouncing": Ibid., 48.